Diversity Training That Generates Real Change

Diversity Training That Generates Real Change

Inclusive Approaches That Benefit Individuals, Business, and Society

James O. Rodgers

Laura L. Kangas

BK

Berrett–Koehler Publishers, Inc.

Berrett-Koehler Publishers, Inc.
1333 Broadway, Suite 1000
Oakland, CA 94612-1921
Tel: (510) 817-2277
Fax: (510) 817-2278
www.bkconnection.com

ORDERING INFORMATION

Quantity sales. Special discounts are available on quantity purchases by corporations, associations, and others. For details, contact the "Special Sales Department" at the Berrett-Koehler address above.

Individual sales. Berrett-Koehler publications are available through most bookstores. They can also be ordered directly from Berrett-Koehler: Tel: (800) 929-2929; Fax: (802) 864-7626; www.bkconnection.com.

Orders for college textbook / course adoption use. Please contact Berrett-Koehler: Tel: (800) 929-2929; Fax: (802) 864-7626.

Distributed to the U.S. trade and internationally by Penguin Random House Publisher Services.

Berrett-Koehler and the BK logo are registered trademarks of Berrett-Koehler Publishers, Inc.

Printed in the United States of America

Berrett-Koehler books are printed on long-lasting acid-free paper. When it is available, we choose paper that has been manufactured by environmentally responsible processes. These may include using trees grown in sustainable forests, incorporating recycled paper, minimizing chlorine in bleaching, or recycling the energy produced at the paper mill.

Library of Congress Cataloging-in-Publication Data

Names: Rodgers, James O., author. | Kangas, Laura L., author.
Title: Diversity training that generates real change : inclusive approaches that benefit individuals,
    business, and society / James O. Rodgers,
  Laura L. Kangas.
Description: First Edition. | Oakland, CA : Berrett-Koehler Publishers,
  [2022] | Includes index.
Identifiers: LCCN 2021062176 (print) | LCCN 2021062177 (ebook) |
  ISBN 9781523001736 (hardcover) | ISBN 9781523001743 (pdf) |
  ISBN 9781523001750 (epub)
Subjects: LCSH: Diversity in the workplace. | Employees—Training of. |
  Personnel management. | Organizational behavior.
Classification: LCC HF5549.5.M5 R628 2022 (print) | LCC HF5549.5.M5
  (ebook) | DDC 658.3008--dc23/eng/20220303
LC record available at https://lccn.loc.gov/2021062176
LC ebook record available at https://lccn.loc.gov/2021062177

First Edition
30 29 28 27 26 25 24 23 22   10 9 8 7 6 5 4 3 2 1

Book production: Tolman Creek Design
Cover design: Alvaro Villanueva, Bookish Design

We, Jim and Laura, dedicate this book to the hundreds
of "old soldiers" who have diligently and consistently
delivered high quality, effective, transformational diversity,
equity and inclusion learning experiences. Thank you for your
commitment to the holy work and the sacred responsibility of
guiding people through personal growth.

I, Laura, also dedicate this book to my parents, Vally
and Waino Kangas, for their love and wisdom; to my daughters,
Savannah and Willow, who remind me every day that
miracles are always a possibility; and to my
paternal grandmother, Lempi Kangas, who helped give
me a "North Star" to believe in.

Contents

Foreword

As an executive coach for over 40 years, my mission for my clients has been to create positive, lasting behavioral change for themselves, their teams, and their organizations. My clients agree that all I teach and coach is easy to understand, but very difficult to do.

My coaching principles are founded on the need for constant repetition of actions and reminders to form new habits. Creating new mindsets and habits requires not only great "lightbulb" moments, but also the thoughtful strategies and planning to rewire a person's default settings over time.

I've seen so many incredibly successful, wealthy, and renowned CEOs be humbled by how difficult it is to make real change in any capacity. It can be so easy to attend a brief seminar, workshop, or start a rigorous plan to change for a week, only to fall back into old habits with the busy nature of life and work. This is the "New Year's Resolution Trap" that makes people believe that by sheer willpower, they will lose the weight, learn a language, or prioritize more time with their families. Without an action plan, accountability, and measurable steps to success, almost everyone gives up their resolution a few weeks into January.

This book is powerfully written and well researched to equip you with the tools you need to create effective Diversity Training that will generate lasting change in your organization. James and Laura will help you create a program or workshop that inspires, and one that sticks with people and drives new habits over a long period of time.

Diversity Training That Generates Real Change dives into the critical components for real change based on the principles of Diversity, Equity, and Inclusion. You'll learn how to communicate the importance of this training for the individual and company, create materials and exercises to engage participants at a profound level, and implement follow-up steps to get back on track as needed.

In my many years working with companies, founders, executives, and managers at every level, I've seen an amazing level of effort to move in the right direction for inclusion and diversity. But there is so much more to be done in this effort. Changing company cultures and organizational systems starts with a shift in behavior for employees throughout a company. There is a need for more awareness of this in the workplace, and for actionable steps to create programs of learning for everyone.

I hope you will read this book and absorb every detail to help make your company a better place for all.

—Marshall Goldsmith
Thinkers 50 #1 Executive Coach and
New York Times bestselling author of
Triggers, Mojo, and *What Got You Here Won't Get You There*

Introduction

What Generates Real Change

What May Be the Best Experience of Your Life

In a conference room at a remote camping facility in rural Alabama, Mike, the CEO of a local gas utility, stood up, went to the front of a class of about 25 people, and said, "Good morning and welcome to what may be the best experience of your life." Mike was a participant in a similar session just months before and was so moved by his experience that he asked Jim if he could attend again. He went on to share his experience with the course and how it had affected his worldview. Then he introduced Jim as a friend, an advisor, and someone who had helped the leaders of the enterprise see the commercial value of becoming a more diversity mature company.

With that setup, Jim confidently said, "What you are about to experience will be different from any training you have had or will have. The main reason is that you are in charge of your learning and what you learn will probably come more from one of your classmates, rather than from me or my co-facilitator." That class of participants included a broad range of diversity dimensions. There were White people, Black people, male and female, highly educated and lower literacy, corporate officers, and frontline operators, and most importantly in Alabama (at the time) both Baptist and Methodist members.

It was clear from people's body language that some of them were willing participants, and some were only there because they were expected to be there. Some of the skeptics relaxed after the very popular CEO spoke. Others became fully engaged after the first learning experience, which taught them that they are equally human, like all the others in the class. That realization created a rich learning environment that benefitted all the participants and led to a better understanding of the human condition.

By the end of the two-day event, there was universal agreement that what participants had shared was a life-affecting, behavior-changing, performance-enhancing, and strategic experience. Over a ten-year period, every employee at that company participated in that experience. The wait list was always extensive. The results were overwhelmingly positive. That is what effective diversity-related training looks like.

What Needs to Be Understood

The soul of diversity work is dangerously close to being lost. Nowhere is that more evident than in the conduct of so-called diversity training. Training is an essential, but by no means a complete, element of a successful diversity, equity, and inclusion (DEI) effort. Since the early development of effective diversity-related training until now, the context and content of the training has devolved from a strategic, change-oriented, personal development investment, into a quick-hit, low-cost, check-the-box activity.

That new focus has proven to be predictably ineffective and resulted in the idea that "diversity training doesn't work." We have been involved in the diversity (management), inclusion, and equity movement since the mid-eighties and have seen the evolution of the field from different vantage points. We hope to show how effective training differs from ineffective training and why it makes more sense for organizations to invest in diversity-related training as part of an overall strategic change effort that results in behavior change.

A Brief History

Diversity management was introduced in an era when Affirmative Action, multiculturalism, pluralism, oppression studies, cross-cultural studies, and race/gender mandates were the order of the day. In this environment, many business enterprises felt conflicted about attending to these social issues or managing their enterprises. It was politically advisable to appear interested in the changing demographics of the country and how well (your) company responded to the needs of new entrants. Still, business performance and social responsiveness seemed like two unconnected and disparate streams of thought, with a clear preference demanded by business performance.

Many corporate leaders suspected that the subtle and incremental changes in the makeup of society would eventually become an important consideration for their firms. That suspicion was confirmed with the 1987 publication of the Workforce 2000 report commissioned by the Department of Labor and conducted by the Hudson Institute. The report predicted that the changes in the makeup of the workforce would be even more dramatic than expected. For example, the finding that by the year 2000, "85% of new entrants to the workforce will be (non-traditional) workers" was the subject of much interpretation, translation, and extrapolation.

Questions such as "What does that mean?" and "What do we need to do?" hung in the air. Many scholars and consultants attempted to answer those questions with varying levels of viability. The most prolific and valuable answer came from a then relatively unknown Harvard-trained scholar from Atlanta, Georgia. Dr. R. Roosevelt Thomas Jr. constructed his response to the new "facts" based on direct observation of his students at Morehouse College and his studies at the University of Chicago and Harvard.

Distilled down, Thomas's original definition of Managing Diversity was: "Managing Diversity is a process for creating an (workplace) environment that naturally allows all employees to contribute fully to the objectives of the organization." He defined diversity as "the collective mix of differences and similarities." The conception of diversity had moved from a matter of social psychology to a matter of enterprise performance.

In the early days of diversity work, we stated that: 1) this is not Affirmative Action, 2) no one should be advantaged to the disadvantage of others, and 3) the goal was enterprise performance. With those principles in mind, the nature of diversity-related training also shifted. It became more focused on behavior change to promote workplace relationships and less about information exchange promoting obscure academic concepts. And it worked—for a while.

About This Book

This book is designed to lead the reader through the life cycle of effective diversity training and highlight the necessary support components to ensure success. These support components include a) tips on how to identify what is less or more effective for long-term DEI change; b) the critical interconnectedness of corporate business strategy, DEI strategy, and diversity training; c) the essential facilitation process, skills, and conditions for DEI behavioral training; d) the need to measure diversity training and DEI strategy in ways that are meaningful, and, e) the call to act with urgency and focus on DEI goals and metrics.

Diversity is not a problem; it is a fact of life. Unfortunately, we have turned this fact of life into one of the most challenging elements of social navigation and enterprise management. This book is for CEOs who feel compelled to promote DEI without truly understanding why, what, or how to do it; it is for politicians who without fully realizing it use the word diversity to make empty promises or to sow seeds of divisiveness. It is for every DEI practitioner in the field who is selling something different and for the millions of advocates who genuinely want to see progress in enterprise performance and social change.

If there is no discipline to how we approach the issue, what we are doing will not be sustainable. What if instead, we could simplify and clarify our response to diversity and create a discipline that could be understood and executed globally and that would produce outcomes that are predictable, replicable, and valuable? We believe that with a minor shift in our perspective and a little thought, we can still deliver on that promise.

Mission

The mission of this book is to help advance diversity, equity, and inclusion (DEI) training across the globe and to make the training authentic, meaningful, and most of all, transformational. The reader will find a practical and easily applicable template for diversity training that generates real change supported by compelling true stories from the field that spotlight successes, challenges, and common missteps. You will journey into the inner workings of world class diversity facilitation. All readers will become better prepared to lead DEI and push back against the opponents of true change that insist that DEI training should be short and cheap. Our hope is that this book will generate a movement across the planet that designs and delivers diversity training that generates real change in individuals, business, and society.

Expectations

This book will provide a template for moving forward, defining the need for behavioral change that will eradicate the impact of destructive "isms" (racism, sexism, colorism, homophobia, etc.)

on workforce relationships and that can accelerate innovation and business success. You will hear stories about real people and their experiences.

Listening is key to learning. As you read this book, listen to the voices of the people in these stories as well as your own voice and the voices of those around you. Our hope is that this book expands your ability to hear all voices, not just those that share your perspective and life experiences.

"Listen to learn and talk to teach" is one of our DEI communication tips. If you practice this approach, a world that you never knew existed can suddenly become visible; we hope you realize that it was there all along and that it took a person different from you to make it real. This is only one of the many valuable learning points that is available to you if you do the DEI work described in this book

We will define terms such as "strategy" and demonstrate how delivering diversity-related training as an element of executing strategy is the better path. Because the audiences for most diversity-related trainings are adults, we follow adult learning theory and illustrate how and why facilitation rather than instruction is more effective. The experiential learning process (the Zen of Facilitation) allows adults to adopt their own learning path with facilitators serving as guides. We keep people safe by creating and managing an environment that avoids a right-wrong orientation.

Overall Goal

The overall goal for effective diversity-related training is a commitment to behavior change and continuous learning. The Six Building Blocks, introduced in Chapter 1 and defined throughout the book, offer a comprehensive path to successful results from DEI training. We support the Six Building Blocks with illustrations of how some companies used these principles and delivered effective learning experiences that contributed to the personal and professional growth of their people. Finally, we will expand on the execution principles outlined and give a call to action to direct the trend towards inclusive DEI training that generates real change and benefits individuals, business, and society across the world.

What We Offer That Is Different

As you read this book, it may be important to understand how we arrived at our point of view about diversity, equity, and inclusion. We have always believed that it is important for us to model the principles of diversity that we invite others to adopt. We (Jim and Laura) certainly exemplify why deliberate use of diverse perspectives is a winning plan.

Jim's Story

I'm an engineer, a business analyst, and (later in life) an academic writer and researcher. I began my career as a fast-track executive candidate in the telecom industry. I worked in nearly every department in that industry including engineering, project management, finance, economics, marketing, sales, and executive development. In several positions, I had profit and loss responsibilities. I began my consulting career working in fields such as total quality management (TQM), career management, and management development. I came into the field of diversity management in an unusual way. My background suggests that I would stay away from anything that smacked of HR or any other non-operations function. I was invited to the field by a senior corporate officer and friend who thought my business focus would add value to the field. I was influenced by the groundbreaking work of Dr. R. Roosevelt Thomas Jr. and have adopted an intention of "promoting the value of diversity while reducing the stigma of diversity."

Three events shaped my philosophy about employee development and corporate training. I was cofounder of the corporate university at BellSouth. I learned from a master teacher named Zyg Nagorski how to use facilitated learning to help adults take ownership of their learning journey. Zyg would often quote Winston Churchill who once said, "I'm always ready to learn, although I do not always like being taught." Rather than instruction, I learned to give adults an opportunity to learn.

In the early ninties, I was the lead facilitator for a program called Changing Times at the Coca-Cola Company. That course was designed by a colleague who trained in Gestalt theory and other adult learning technologies. During the program, I saw adults open up, be introspective, and share openly with a classroom full of fellow employees. The depth of learning and the application of ideas to everyday work-life was impressive. That course used the experiential learning model, Experience—Discovery—Implication—Application, which has since been a staple of my designs.

Finally, I was influenced by the design and delivery process on the Texaco project, which Laura will describe in Chapter 8. I was both a member of the faculty and the lead consultant in the Upstream organization (exploration and production) in Houston. I saw how a carefully designed learning experience coupled with expert advice and counsel about strategy execution could influence business outcomes.

I must add that as a spiritual teacher, I see direct parallels between ancient spiritual wisdom and the challenges we face in organizational life. I do not hesitate to make those connections when appropriate.

I came to training as a secondary part of my value proposition, behind consulting, advice, and counsel. My philosophy about effective diversity-related training comes from years of direct experience, not from theory or speculation. I have personally designed over thirty unique learning experiences as part of diversity change efforts and have successfully managed delivery to hundreds of thousands of employees using the principles in this book.

Laura's Story

In many ways I (Laura) was born into the work of diversity, equity, and inclusion. My grandparents, who were all immigrants, were involved in the American labor movement in the 1920s. My paternal grandmother was head of the "Workers' Council," fighting for child labor laws, safety in the mills, and twelve-hour workdays. She was called in one day to the head boss's office, along with other Council members, and was told that they had all lost their jobs. Because it was a "mill town," she could not get another job because their names were put on a "list" (black-listed) that did not allow anyone in the town to hire them.

This story is told with great pride in our family, as well as the part that includes the fact that subsequently my grandparents' home was shot at, and the only employment that my grandmother could get was as a cook and a maid in a neighboring town that allowed her to come home one night a week to see her husband and two young sons. The sentiment I always remember, and that guides my life, is that there are things worth fighting for, even worth making sacrifices for in the short run, for a longer-term, broader gain. In my mind, the 21st century version of diversity, equity, and inclusion deserves the same dedication and spirit that drove the American workers' movement in the 1920s.

As a young child, I was heavily impacted by the Civil Rights movement, and especially by the words and pictures of Dr. Martin Luther King Jr. I regularly cut quotes out of the daily newspaper and Life magazine representing the Civil Rights work that so many were doing. I pasted those pictures and quotes on my side of the sliding closet door of the bedroom that I shared with my sister Arlene. My parents kept them there for many years.

As an internal Senior Human Resource Business Consultant supporting over 700 employees in my early days in the corporate world, I attended many of the pioneering sessions of diversity, equity, and inclusion training. I knew that the principles of diversity, equity and inclusion were solid and the right thing to do for our employees and the business. The silver lining of the recession of the 1980s was that I got an opportunity to design a program in-house and, as they say, the rest is history.

Our design and facilitation team designed and delivered a two-day experiential-based DEI training workshop that changed peoples' lives in a meaningful and powerful way. The training, supported by the company's DEI strategy, executive leadership, and many DEI learning opportunities, was delivered to over 125,000 employees, many of whom formed friendships that have continued to this day.

Through my own consulting company, I have been blessed with opportunities to do similar DEI work all over the world. I have spent many years on the frontline, living, breathing, and creating the work of DEI. It has been such a privilege to be involved in what I consider "sacred work," whose value and findings Jim and I want to share with the world. Honestly, I never thought the vast majority of my work life would be spent in the corporate setting, but then one day I had an "epiphany" of sorts. I realized that corporations are in a unique position to help change people's lives and the world. Almost everyone needs a job. Imagine if we could make real change that would impact not only this generation, but all the ones to come, on a global level.

What also fuels my passion about DEI work is the spirit and growth of people along the way, witnessing their learning, and growing in front of my eyes. I know that long-lasting DEI behavioral change and impact can happen. I have experienced it in myself and in so many others.

The Problem Beneath the Problem (What Is the Objective?)

The assertion that diversity-related training does not work misses one important factor. Have you decided what "works" looks like? The explicit objectives of some diversity-related training include numerous expectations such as rectifying DEI concerns, improving employee morale, increasing collaboration, fostering free exchange of ideas, and enhancing the hiring retention and promotion of diverse candidates. We are not aware of any training that can accomplish those objectives on its own.

Unrealistic expectations (unclear objectives) have fed into negative press about the failure of diversity training. Much of that trend is connected to the advent of internal diversity practitioners with small budgets and little experience with effective change efforts. To see why diversity-related training has lost its effectiveness, we will explore its evolution and examine in detail what we mean when we say our training works. Setting and meeting clear objectives is the key to any successful initiative and it is especially true in the field of diversity, equity, and inclusion.

You cannot skip the hours of focused training in any field and expect excellence. Imagine an amateur athlete or new finance manager who receives training, but needs to ask questions, practice, and fully integrate the information into behavioral change to reap the benefits. We can understand the urgency of wanting instant results from DEI training but there are no shortcuts or "silver bullets." Many organizations have learned this truth the hard way. They wasted valuable time and money because of the shortcomings of what they call their "Diversity Training initiatives." At best, many off-the-shelf DEI courses are designed to make people aware and conversant about DEI issues. These materials will educate, but not motivate; inform, but not transform. Successful diversity-related training needs to be carefully linked to enterprise strategy and support the development of DEI skills that will create behavioral change to improve unique workplace cultures.

What Are We Talking About

A DEI effort is a change effort. A change effort involves a number of specific elements to create a more effective organization. Training is a part of it, but many elements are needed to make change sustainable. Diversity training works when it supports the objectives of the change effort and the strategy that prompted the change in the first place. We cannot expect training to bear the entire burden for success of the effort. We need some perspective.

While diversity training is not the end-all of a diversity program, it is the most visible element of the process. When it is done well and has a positive spin in a company, it can put a glow on the other elements of the change process. When it is not done well and has a negative spin, it can derail the entire initiative. It is worth the effort to make sure diversity-related training is successful and that it delivers on the objectives set forth by the leaders of the enterprise. The good news is that well-designed, effective, and successful diversity-related training is well within your reach. We want to show you how to do it.

Foundational Training Is for Everyone

Effective foundational diversity training requires that all participants feel they are on equal footing with the other participants. For that reason, we recommend as one of the group norms we present an agreement of "Hats Off" (everyone is equal despite gender, race, level, function, or title). The class cohorts are meant to include a broad range of diversity dimensions. In our model, the CEO will be in a session with a frontline operator, a middle manager, a janitor, a secretary, and people from every other function in the business. It is important that rank not affect the process of introspection and reflection and that no one withholds their voice for fear of reaction from a higher up.

We also believe that it is not useful for executives to assume that diversity training is good for their people but not for them. Once we make it clear that everyone is included in the participant pool, it changes the dynamics and expectations of the training. Part of the effectiveness of diversity training is the attitude that participants bring to the experience. One of the most frequent comments that people have about principle-centered training with impact is "if only my manager (or boss) could experience this." In our model, their boss has experienced or will experience it.

How to Establish Clear Objectives

The objectives of diversity-related training should mirror the objectives of the overall diversity initiative. The best way to confirm the objectives of the diversity initiative is to do a thorough assessment. In our model, we use a three-phase consulting process. It includes assessment, visioning, and learning.

A comprehensive organizational assessment helps the consulting practitioner and the training designer determine what are the major issues to be addressed. It may consist of a diversity readiness assessment and a culture assessment. Diversity readiness is a careful review of employee attitudes and opinions about issues of employee and market diversity. We usually conduct focus groups, executive interviews, and readiness surveys to determine the general sense of need for a diversity intervention.

Common Traits of Ineffective Diversity Training

The table below illustrates some of the common traits of ineffective training compared with the traits of more effective training. For change to occur, you need to be clear about good intentions with poor outcomes. It is good that leaders recognize that diversity-related training is an essential element of successful workplace management in the 21st century. It would be better if those leaders extended the effort to make sure that what they offered met the urgent need of equipping all employees with a mindset that accounts for the new reality (increasing diversity) and the skills and behaviors to make the workplace more inclusive and productive.

Common Traits of Ineffective Diversity Training

Doesn't Work	Works
Instruction	Facilitation (Zen)
Targeted audiences (need to be fixed)	Full audience (need to be equipped)
Shaming and blaming	Personal introspection
Information exchange	Experiential learning
Awareness and sensitivity	Commitment to behavior change
Prepackages (generic)	Custom and specific to company
Trainer-centric	Learner-centric
Non-strategic	Tied to strategy
Focus on theory	Focus on practice
Low-cost decision point	Strategic investment
Mandated "have to" event	Valued "want to" experience
Check the box	Outcome-focused
One-off event	Long-term change

Pure instruction can elicit one of two reactions. Either the participant will seek to win by mastering the topic more than others (I got a 100% on the quiz) or they will resent being told how to think and feel about topics which are so emotional, personal, and seemingly punitive. Just the idea that someone from the outside wants to tell us we are wrong is offensive.

Targeted audiences further exacerbate the feeling that the trainer is here to "fix" me. When training is focused solely on managers, or past offenders, or White men in particular, it creates a stigma associated with an assumption that someone needed correction.

Even in a mixed audience, any sense of shaming and blaming isn't well received. Strategic training has to remove any sense that anyone or any group is isolated as the villain. The fact is that the word "diversity" has come to mean for many a reference to race and gender differences. Trainers must not reinforce that notion by giving examples of, for instance, how White men have oppressed others, or how men have denigrated women, or any "us vs. them" comparison. In our model, there are no good guys; there are no bad guys; there are only humans who all suffer from the same types of personal and group responses.

Research has shown how little shared information is retained when one person informs another. There is a wealth of emerging information about racism, genderism, bias, prejudice, stereotypes, brain mechanics, discrimination, tribalism, and any number of other concepts that relate to the reality of an increasingly diverse society. Many times, participants are led to learn an ever-expanding lexicon of diversity-related terms. Information exchange is fraught with opportunities for ineffectiveness. We have learned that attendance does not mean participation; participation does not assume learning; learning does not ensure retention; and retention does not guarantee change. People have to have a reason to engage with new information. Please note: their reason will not likely be your reason.

Awareness and sensitivity are the main topics in many diversity trainings. Awareness cannot be confined to a litany of data and information. As mentioned earlier, information exchange is not likely to produce any meaningful change. Sensitivity also cannot be imposed. It must be felt. The participant who really benefits from sensitivity must have their own reason for internalizing it.

Prepackaged, standard, or generic training programs are not specific to any company's needs or culture. They can give the impression that some outside entity is telling the company how to think, feel, and act. It also implies that they have been doing things wrong all along. Generic means the trainers will not use language that is familiar to participants and will introduce concepts that have no immediate application in their workplace.

Who is in charge of learning in the classroom? For a trainer-directed program it is the trainer. The trainer comes in with a set of content and an agenda. They are judged on their ability to cover that agenda despite what comes up in the session. That may serve the needs of the trainer but does not necessarily serve the needs of the participants.

Executing strategy requires that a person first understand what strategy means. Many practitioners, both internal and external, are not aware of the meaning or the implication of calling something strategic. Effective diversity training should be directly related to the specific organizational objectives and the specific task each team member is responsible for. There should be a direct connection between the principles learned in the classroom and the requirements in the workplace. Failure to do so makes training predictably ineffective.

One of the frequent traps that trainers fall into is to latch onto the latest theoretical concepts coming out of the academy.

Requiring people to become doctoral level students of esoteric concepts is not a winning formula. There is a difference between theory and practice. Diversity-related training should be a practical exercise.

The decision of how to handle the training component of a diversity initiative is an important decision. It should not be solely based on cost. If you see diversity training as a cost or expense, you will probably opt for the lowest cost option available. The lowest cost option is rarely the best option.

Mandated training has a special stigma attached to it. Leaders should be wary of mandating that people attend diversity-related training. Instead, particularly in a strong culture, everyone should be encouraged and specifically invited to participate in the session. Participants have to enter the training in the right state of mind for it to be effective.

What is your motivation for conducting diversity related training? If you do not have a clear business objective, you are probably just checking the box to make it appear that you have a serious interest in becoming more diversity mature. That seldom leads to success.

Finally, if diversity-related training is treated as a singular, isolated, one-off event it will predictably not be effective. Conducting training as a way of saying we are doing something about diversity is simply a waste of money, time, and resources.

Understanding Strategy

Strategy, by definition, is the position a company must hold in order to win. Every organizational strategy has a people component. Part of a people strategy is the recognition that employees come in all types and dimensions of diversity. The human capital component of any strategy includes things such as who we are, how we manage people, and how we make them feel. That positioning can set a company apart and make it more attractive to potential employees. Understanding human behavior is important in getting people to work together more productively. A portion of each training session should be dedicated to highlighting the organizational strategy that undergirds the need for the training. Training to strategy changes the dynamics of the learning environment. People are more likely to want to learn in order to be equipped to thrive in the evolving corporate environment rather than being taught how they need to be fixed.

Facilitation (Zen)—the Art and Science of Delivery

The two factors that have the biggest impact on effective diversity-related training are superior facilitators and the design of the exercises. Facilitators are more than trainers. Facilitation is both a natural and an acquired skill set. DEI facilitators must be able to facilitate difficult conversations without imputing their own bias and conditioning into the dialogue. DEI facilitators are asked to guide people through exercises that involve deep reflection and personal introspection. There are no pat answers.

The Facilitation Zen requires practitioners to focus on the other participants and not themselves. They must also have an innate understanding of and compassion for human nature. A skilled and effective DEI facilitator will have examined their own belief system and will have become attuned to their personal hot buttons. They are not required to abandon who they are; instead, they are called on to model the ability to manage the impact of their hot buttons, biases, prejudices, and stereotypes. That ability begins with an examination of "self," which is an intense personal exercise, yet one that is necessary before taking on the sacred responsibility of DEI facilitation. If participants feel like the facilitators are pushing their own agenda and beliefs, they tend to shut down and resist. Master facilitation can avoid that trap.

Is It Safe to Open Up?

The core definition of diversity management is "creating an environment that allows everyone to contribute fully to the objectives of the organization." The core requirement of effective diversity-related training is creating an environment in which everyone's story is of equal value. Creating a safe space demands more than being emotionally supportive; it requires adherence to the principle that all humans are equally subject to the traps of unconscious discrimination based solely on our shared humanity. A safe space is an environment where everyone is validated and encouraged to state their truth without fear of denigration or ridicule. In some types of diversity training, members of the majority (dominant) culture are told to listen to and validate the perspectives of minority (marginalized) groups. At the same time, they are asked to submit their own feelings and perspectives to intense scrutiny. This sets up a clear double standard which does not feel safe to anyone.

Adults already live in a world where they face shame, blame, stigma, social discord, and confusion. Paul Bracy, a gifted colleague, often comments at the start of a session that "No one here created this condition. We were all born into it." Set-ups like that can help even the playing field of exploration so that no one feels disadvantaged to the advantage of others. It avoids having members of the dominant group walking away believing that they, their culture, their perspectives, and their interests are not valued at the institution. This approach avoids an "us vs. them" attitude in which minority groups are seen as fragile and easily offended. That uneven posture makes it more difficult for people to build relationships and collaborate across differences.

A successful diversity training session has to create an environment of meritocracy of pain. We all have pain. No one is exempt. Diversity training should be the great equalizer—it cannot focus on whose pain is greater. Recognizing that fact can be the basis of a mutual bond that can lead to sustainable change in behavior toward each other. Conversations should include all dimensions of diversity.

Experiencing Experiential Learning

Immediately after exposing participants to the experiential learning model that is Experience, Discovery, Implication, Application, we begin with an experience that illustrates the learning process for the entire Learning Experience. The intent of this initial exercise is to defuse any notions that "Sure, these people may have problems with diversity, but not me." An example is a classic training game called the "F Card." The idea is that inherently, humans are conditioned to see some things and not others. Even the most careful and thoughtful player will discover that they have overlooked something.

This is one of many games that trainers play that can defuse a reluctance to learn. The difference in this case is in how the class leader processes the experience. A competent trainer ends the exercise by telling the class what the experience meant. A superior facilitator would instead end the exercise by asking the class what it meant to them personally. What did they discover? The class responds using their language, their insights, and their perspectives.

Experiential training as the primary delivery modality allows all participants to consider how they naturally respond to other people and other situations. We invite them to consider new thinking and new behavior, but for their own reasons. They are free to adopt new ideas that are important to them rather than being told what ideas are important to us.

Are You Sure This Works?

How do you know if you have been successful with any training effort? Experiment and test behaviors constantly. The assessment process has to be rather robust. In our model, we ask participants if they allowed for movement in their point of view, if they discovered anything of value to their personal perspective, if they felt we covered all the areas we discussed at the opening, and if they are committed to continuous learning about people. What else would you expect from a training session?

We ask managers to support new behaviors by articulating the principles outlined in the training. Training is a catalyst for organizational change. Ultimately people own the responsibility for change. If you invest in effective training, effective training will help them accelerate that change.

In a Nutshell, What Generates Real Change?

Here is a summary of the traits of diversity training that work:

- Rather than instruction, sessions should be conducted as facilitated learning experiences. Learning guided by a Zen facilitator can provide comfort.
- Rather than single out specific people or groups to take the training, make it a shared experience for all employees from frontline to CEO.
- Rather than picking on some participants for historical disparities for which they are not responsible, allow all participants to do their own personal reflection without scrutiny.
- Rather than simply sharing facts and data about what you want people to learn, give them room to learn what they want to learn.

- Rather than limiting the content to awareness and sensitivity, equip participants for behavior change that will affect relationships.
- Rather than a cheap, generic, off-the-shelf training package, design and deliver an experience that is unique and specific to your company.
- Rather than following a trainer's agenda, allow participants to decide what they learn.
- Rather than present something unrelated to the company's strategy, tie the training content directly to the execution of strategy.
- Rather than latching onto the latest academic theory, maintain a practical element to the training.
- Rather than spending on the cost of training, invest in development and change.
- Rather than making people attend a useless event, invite them, and encourage them to participate in a value-added experience.
- Rather than simply checking the box, focus on specific results-oriented outcomes.
- Rather than executing a quick-hit, unrelated event, develop a change process that includes training and ongoing reinforcement.

The Urgency of Time

The business world and the planet are crying out to make significant DEI changes. Together, with greater knowledge and wisdom, we can do this. As a result, we will gain the wisdom to create more inclusive workplaces that allow talent to shine and businesses to prosper even more.

Don't Leave Me Hanging

So, once you know everything that is laid out in this book, what are you expected to do or to stop doing? It begins with confirming why you are interested in diversity training in the first place. If the answer is, "Because everyone else is doing it," you are probably not going to get value for your money and effort. We suggest that you follow a few simple steps:

- Back up and rethink your diversity initiative
- Think more strategically about how this fits your overall corporate strategy
- Invest in training that works
- Presell the idea so that your employees understand the "why"
- Make the focus on personal growth and behavior change
- Get competent experienced help, this is not for amateurs
- Conduct a culture analysis
- Be clear about the desired outcomes
- Make it cool to participate and uncool to not participate
- Reinforce the learning with new behavioral expectations on the job

Follow these tips, read the rest of the book, reference it often, and you will experience *diversity training that generates real change.*

Chapter 1

Diversity, Equity, and Inclusion
What's Training Got to Do with It?

"Not everything that is faced can be changed but nothing can be changed that is not faced."

—James Baldwin

Intellectual conversation around diversity and inclusion rarely, if ever, creates behavioral change. Articles, books, videos, e-learning modules, and other materials can be useful as tools to support diversity and inclusion work. Without making an emotional connection to the work and gaining a deep understanding and acknowledgement of the added value to one's personal and work life success, the training remains merely an intellectual conversation, and nothing changes.

Tragically, this is the fate of too many well-intentioned DEI trainings that have been delivered over the past thirty years. It is a seductive process because it is easy to do, receives very little pushback from most participants (for various reasons), is relatively inexpensive, and can be pointed to as evidence that "we are an organization that values diversity."

It doesn't work because an emotional connection to diversity, equity, and inclusion has not been made, and the hard work of coming to grips with your personal "unconscious bias" and "blind spots" never happened. In some ways, diversity training gives people a "pass." For example, if you complete the e-learning module, check the box, and fail *to identify explicit value or accountability for diversity-related behaviors in the organization, you have produced effort without outcomes. Personal/emotional connection is essential. It also needs to be supported by a DEI organizational strategy; without clarity around the relevance and applicability of the learning to the organization's success, diversity training is doomed to failure.*

There Is a Difference

An inspired mechanical engineer once proclaimed that her company did diversity training. When questioned about what it involved, she explained it was an annual one-hour online program that defined the terms. When asked if it had impacted her behavior and/or changed anything in the organization, she responded, "No, but it is nice to be informed. And besides, we are very busy." In our experience, this type of diversity, equity, and inclusion training doesn't work. It lacks a human connection.

A very different example and outcome was shared by an assistant professor from the Harvard Kennedy School of Government who writes about an experience of delivering a diversity, equity, and inclusion training session to primarily White police officers. The assistant professor came very well prepared with DEI research findings, statistical data, and other written documentation, but rather quickly observed that it was creating very little response from the group.

He was mystified and disappointed at the lack of interest. There was no meaningful dialogue on how to make things better concerning DEI in the organization and no discussion about the challenges and problems that were clearly identified by the data. That is, until a Black police officer began to speak about the information. The Black officer simply stated with emotion and powerful authenticity, "This is my life, this is the life that I have been living."

The assistant professor put down his notes and his training outline. He reported that when that human connection was made, the dynamics of the session changed. White officers began to listen with great intensity. The group began to have authentic and meaningful conversations about their own and others' life experiences.

Having reached a greater level of trust, the group reached a new level of DEI awareness. That awareness motivated the group to authentically consider and publicly commit to what they could do better. They began to plan how to make the organization more effective and how to benefit the community. That day was a significant step in the DEI journey for the members of the police force. The training session significantly influenced how seriously the organization considered the DEI strategy that they later developed. That plan benefitted the individuals, the organization, and ultimately, society.

Why Training?

Diversity, equity, and inclusion are a set of principles designed to help an organization perform better by equipping the people with an awareness and a skillset to promote stronger, more productive, more comfortable relationships. For many organizations with large numbers of employees and customers, DEI involves a retooling of fundamental skills, attitudes, and knowledge. It is a strategy and a capability that sets people up for success and competitive advantage. Doing it right involves a large-scale change initiative that includes everyone in the organization.

From an organizational development (OD) standpoint, change initiatives involve several steps and touchpoints to define the change, prepare for the change, install the change, and monitor how well the change is sticking. Of all the steps in a change effort, training is the most important. Leaders set the strategy, project managers manage the process, and external advisors help provide objective guidance, but managers and regular people make it happen.

Training is the linchpin of a large-scale change initiative regarding DEI for three reasons.

- First, it is the most visible of all the project components. When people see and hear about executives, managers, and all their fellow employees having a shared experience, it signals to them that something important is up.

- Second, it is the most personal. It is a shared experience, but everyone has their own personal learning journey in the process.

- Finally, it produces the most profound change at the individual and team level. As seasoned facilitators, we have been blessed to bear witness to thousands of cathartic events, moments of awakening, and life-changing epiphanies during DEI sessions. It is designed as a business event, but has implications for every aspect of a person's life.

Which Diversity Training?

Most commentators speak of diversity-related training as though it were a singular event or standard course. In our experience there are many different versions of diversity-related training designed for different reasons and with different outcomes. Here are some:

Executive education is designed to help enterprise leaders consider if and how a DEI effort (including training) is right for them at this time. The focus is on definitions, strategy, possibilities, and examples of successful outcomes. This is mostly a guided discussion session with a commitment question at the end.

Management training with a DEI focus is designed to give frontline managers a chance to consider how their role in managing the frontline "value creators" is critical to success with DEI. The focus is on promoting knowledge of the broad range of perspectives available to them for doing the important work of the enterprise. It also promotes the idea that it is management more than leadership that leads to success with DEI.

Marketing and sales events with a DEI focus are designed to help customer-facing employees understand how they may be leaving money on the table by not managing their diversity response. These sessions have changed marketing foci and sales tactics and expanded the success patterns for many enterprises.

HR and compliance training sessions are designed to help human capital professionals learn how they can be supportive of frontline managers and employees as they try to work more productively with an increasingly diverse employee base.

Deliberate diversity training is a targeted learning experience designed to guide managers through an experimentation process to discover if and how a more diverse team can deliver better results than a more homogeneous team.

Foundational training is designed to equip all employees with the basic understanding of the natural human response to increasing diversity. It is presented often as sensitivity and awareness training, but is increasingly presented as a strategy and competency (skills) learning experience. This is the level of training that is most often being referred to as diversity training. We will focus most of our comments on this level of the process.

The Building Blocks

There is a logical methodical process for delivering foundational diversity training that generates change. This book is laid out to address each step of that process. Each building block supports and is supported by the other steps. They are not as much steps as they are touchpoints. Successful DEI projects always include these touchpoints as part of their strategy and execution plan.

These Six Building Blocks help to create successful diversity learning experiences in support of an effective DEI change effort.

Building Block 1 (Chapter 2)	Know Your Why
Building Block 2 (Chapter 3)	Know Your Strategy
Building Block 3 (Chapter 4)	Know Your Audience (Adults)
Building Block 4 (Chapter 5)	Know How to Deliver (Facilitation)
Building Block 5 (Chapter 6)	Know the Learning Model
Building Block 6 (Chapter 7)	Know Your Execution Plan

A plan that includes all these touchpoints will have a greater prospect for creating an environment where everyone feels comfortable and productive in support of organizational objectives.

Does It Promote Relationships?

Diversity management is a relationship discipline. All humans see some differences in other humans, yet too often we let these differences distract us and become a barrier to effective relationships instead of a source for learning, perspective, and enhanced understanding. Conversely, all humans can find things in common with all other humans, and those similarities can be the catalyst for more comfortable and productive relationships.

The development of any discipline begins with clearly defining the problem. In the case of diversity management, the problem is how to manage the distractions caused by differences. It takes intention and skills to overcome that natural human tendency. Good DEI training should equip people to "seek similarities" with others so that their differences matter less. Productive relationships are the desired outcome.

The Goal

The goal of diversity-related training is to help people see other people as equal in value and humanity, and as sacred spirits with varying competencies, life experiences, creative and spiritual gifts. That translates into people with brown skin seeing people with white skin as equals, not as superior, not as more biased, not as an "up." Likewise, a person with white skin should learn to see a person with brown skin as equal, not as inferior, not as poor, disadvantaged, under-represented, marginalized—not as a "down." In his landmark book, *The Nature of Prejudice*, Gordon Allport, talked about prejudice as "being down on what you are not up on."

On their face, the goals outlined above seem simple, logical, and common sense. The one thing that complicates the execution of those goals is the human condition. The human condition is the result of human conditioning—socialization and self-protection instincts, which if left unchecked, would cause humans to remain as savage and unsophisticated as any other animal on the planet. We all have acquired bias, learned prejudice, a collection of stereotypes, and a natural reaction to differences. For the goals to be achieved, however, we must find a way to address the impact of our human conditioning. We must make better decisions about people. We must learn to think before we react.

The Context

The Short and Quick Approach (Doesn't Work)

Intellectual conversations about DEI rarely, if ever, create behavioral change. Articles, books, videos, e-learning modules, guest speakers and other materials can be useful as tools to support and inform people about diversity, equity, and inclusion work, but they rarely generate long-lasting and deeply rooted behavioral and organizational change. The *Harvard Business Review* reports that the term "diversity fatigue" has been coined to describe diversity, equity, and inclusion efforts that are empty words without follow-up actions that "are simply for face value." At best these efforts inform people, but rarely, if ever, transform individuals, businesses, or society.

In addition, many of these so-called DEI training efforts are essentially DEI support materials, which are often focused on a specific dimension of diversity sometimes referred to as "the flavor of the month." That approach often leaves others feeling excluded, invisible, and not valued. It can also generate resentment in other peoples' minds, with questions like: "What about me and my group?" These approaches lack the inclusive focus that genuine DEI programs need to have as their foundation. Again, *informational*, but *rarely transformational*.

The Emotional Connection

DEI training that gives participants an opportunity to talk and hear each other's stories can create a human connection. The human connection leads to an emotional awareness that generates action and change. Without an emotional connection, DEI training remains at the intellectual level. Rarely does anything even slightly change. It is a seductive process because informational training is easy to do, it receives very little negative pushback from participants, it is relatively inexpensive, and it can be misused as evidence to publicly proclaim that the organization values diversity.

(Laura) In an exercise where participants discussed and listed stereotypes about different dimensions of diversity, we acknowledged the stark reality that different places in the world contain different stereotypes depending on history, events, etc.

The participants then stood in front of the list that gave them a "charge." A charge is defined as an emotional response to the list. It may be positive or negative. They were then asked to share with the group why they selected that particular list.

The plant manager was the last to go and was clearly hesitating on selecting a list. The room grew silent. The manager was known to be a powerful, wealthy, privileged White male with an Ivy League degree. People wondered aloud, "What type of diversity challenges could he possibly have?" Slowly the plant manager walked over to the chart that listed the stereotypes about Vietnam veterans. A profound silence came over the room as he turned to the group with a look of sadness on his face and tears in his eyes, and said, "I am a Vietnam veteran and I have never told that to anyone in this company because I know the stereotypes that are out there about Vietnam vets".

"People think we are crazy, baby killers, mentally ill, and suffer from PTSD. I know that I would have been looked at differently if people knew that I was a Vietnam vet. I have kept it hidden until this moment. I decided to say it now because I just realized that there are people in this room, this company, and in the world that suffer every day because they get judged, stereotyped, and labeled for elements of diversity that they can't hide. I could hide mine, and have done so, because I knew the potential consequences. I never looked at it this way before and I am deeply sorry."

The plant manager later told us that without the DEI training experience, he never would have become the diversity champion that he grew into. Nor would he have developed the deep awareness and healing he needed for his own wounds. The fact that the training included meaningful interactions with others and the unique opportunity to connect with others as humans made all the difference.

He went on to talk with the group about his experiences when he returned from Vietnam. He was spat at. He had, on some level, judged himself all these years even though he knew that he had made an honorable decision to enlist. Some class members told him that they appreciated his courage and were sorry for his pain and suffering. Some other class members were Vietnam refugees and were able to tell him their perspective. Others, who had not been directly impacted by the Vietnam War, shared their perspective. Everyone in the room that day broadened and deepened their understanding that we are all in this together. Everyone has pain. Everyone has a story. Everyone needs to be part of the DEI conversation.

Finding the Missing Connection

The fact is, we don't know what any other person has experienced in life. Nor do we know what affects another person. If we rely only on what we think about a person, we may miss the opportunity for genuine connection.

(Laura) John was a financially secure, White male, senior manager in his early fifties who sat wrapped in a tightly fastened tan raincoat for almost two days in one of our multi-day training sessions, only engaging in conversation when necessary. We respected his space and privately checked in with him regularly.

Moved by the authentic and generous sharing of stories by others, in the early afternoon of the second day, he suddenly began to talk about his pain of not being able to relate to women. He admitted to always feeling defensive and devalued for being born a White man. He was angry that his leisure-time activities, such as belonging to a yacht club, were now being "infiltrated" (his words, not ours) by women.

Clearly distraught, he did not know what to do and asked for help. We did not know this man personally, so we did not have any idea how long he had been carrying these feelings. But it was evident that it was impacting his professional success and personal life. This illustrates the power of the human connection in

DEI training. Others listened to his story without judgment and helped him figure out who the enemy was (not women), how to move through his fear, and to begin to open his life to different dimensions of diversity. Participants talked with him about opening his personal and professional life to many new and exciting opportunities without totally giving up anything that he deeply cherished.

The Power of Inclusive Approaches

Effective diversity training cannot be done in a vacuum. The invitation to be part of the diversity, equity and inclusion conversation must be all-inclusive and empathy must be extended to all. DEI training needs to be a space where all dimensions of diversity are welcome and valued, and everyone's story and experience is listened to and respected for its human connection. Otherwise, you are setting up yourself and the organization for failure.

What Training Can Contribute

If you agree with the ideas and concepts of diversity, equity, and inclusion, training is a useful tool. Diversity training does three things:

(1) Gives space for adults to come to their own understanding and awareness of all aspects of DEI, including how it has impacted their own and others' lives.

(2) Helps participants make a business connection to how DEI can enhance and improve their business.

(3) Helps participants understand how their actions as individuals impact themselves, the businesses they work for, and society at large in a profound way. It affects their personal and professional lives.

Two Key Elements

Diversity training that benefits individuals, businesses, and society must have at least two important elements:

1. **The training must spark a human connection between people in the session**.

    Through the sharing of diversity-related life experiences, people begin to realize how much they do not know about other peoples' lives. That realization often comes with a powerful jolt to their consciousness. A window is opened to an expanded awareness of the impact of diversity, equity, and inclusion on an individual's personal and professional lives. They begin to visualize images of people attached to the concepts they are reviewing.

    They see real people whose daily professional and personal lives are deeply impacted by the DEI statistics they read and the news stories they have heard. Through this process, the connection to one's own life becomes much clearer, which can create breakthrough moments in an individual's DEI journey. Perhaps their own stories have never been told, and/or did not fit the types of stories that were most often discussed in relation to DEI. However, their story had been deeply impactful in their own life experience. Perhaps people feared that their stories would not be viewed as politically correct, worthy of discussion, and emotionally connected to DEI work as others saw it.

    This "missing connection" is often uncovered dramatically in participants of our multiday workshops. Diversity, equity, and inclusion is rarely the problem preventing the authentic acceptance and development of relationships with others, but so often it is used as an easy target to blame. Training that fuels human connection is essential for real change to happen whether it is at the individual, organizational, or societal level.

2. **The training must be totally and equally inclusive of all dimensions of diversity.**

People don't need to agree with everyone's views, but the respect and acceptance of their humanness in a diversity training is non-negotiable. Growth in diversity, equity, and inclusion training does not come from keeping some dimensions of diversity invisible and undiscussable. This action negates the commitment of everything that diversity, equity, and inclusion training stands for. The more we can intentionally listen to each other, rather than judging and/or prematurely deciding we know what is true for them and not getting defensive ourselves, the more opportunity we will have to learn and be better partners and leaders in DEI.

The Diversity Lens

A priceless value of diversity training based on human connection is that it creates an opportunity for individuals to have the type of unique and necessary moments of diversity awareness that generate behavior change. We often talk about diversity training that generates change as creating a "diversity lens" through which you can never look at the world in quite the same way again. It can be stunning to realize new things about yourself and others concerning diversity, equity, and inclusion. We often talk about this as a "DEI moment," when you look in the mirror and may not like what you see.

These moments of DEI awareness can include seeing and realizing things about how much you have been missing, how your past behaviors and words may have impacted others, the biases that you may have, and how much you really do not know about DEI that you perhaps thought that you did. Not to worry—in diversity, equity, and inclusion work, we honor and celebrate these moments of awareness because it is a great place to begin to learn what we don't know about others and ourselves. This is the type of inclusive approach to DEI training that we need to be doing as a critical part of DEI programs within our organizations if we are to be successful.

Understanding You and Me

The hard work of understanding your own and others' DEI challenges is a critical part of diversity training that generates real change. Ineffective training too often gives people and organizations a pass. For example, if you complete the e-learning module, check the box, and fail to identify explicit value or accountability for diversity-related behaviors in the organization, you have produced effort without outcomes.

Personal and emotional connection is essential. These emotional connections need to be supported by organizational strategy and behavioral norms. Without clarity around the relevance and applicability of the learning to the organization's success, diversity training is doomed to failure.

How Obi Taught Me Jedi Magic

Laura shared a story that illustrates how we all have been affected by our unique set of life experiences.

(Laura) I used to say that I disliked dogs. Sometimes in my fear I would even say that I hated dogs. On the very rare occasions when I got to know someone's friendly dog, I would make an exception. Then I would go on to explain to anyone who would listen that, "I have been bitten three times by dogs whose owners had said to me that their dogs were friendly." I would feel very justified and self-righteous about what I had said about dogs and my fear of dogs. It made perfect sense to me.

Then one day, our family got a dog, and my world changed. My younger daughter Willow had been wanting a dog ever since she could speak. Finally, shortly before she turned twenty-one years old, I realized I would be very sad if Willow never got to have a dog. So, we got her a dog. What you need to know is that three days after we got Willow's dog that she named Obi, (yes, *Star Wars* fans, it is a reference to Obi-Wan Kenobi, Jedi Master), she went in for knee surgery. For almost three weeks, I was responsible for Obi. I had to face my fears "up close and personal."

Obi and I had lots of time to get to know each other. In many ways, we walked through the "DEI fire" together. Our neighbor, Kate, seeing the diversity challenge, gave us a gift of a "dog-whisperer trainer." I was deeply humbled while working with the trainer. The gift that I received was that I realized that it wasn't dogs that I had a problem with, it was with the owners who did not properly train their dogs. I realized that my angst and distrust was misplaced, and my former behavior was misdirected. I could not have learned this without living through it. I was so sure that I was right about dogs, and I had several examples to prove it (I even have a scar!).

Here's what I came to know. Dogs are basically wonderful animals, pets, and companions. It is the owners that can mess them up. The early morning walks in the rain, navigating busy streets, and the opportunity to live day-to-day with a dog transformed me. I realized how truly wonderful our dog Obi was and how unconsciously incompetently (badly) I had treated him. Yet, Obi stuck with me, did everything that I asked, and in some ways, gave more than I deserved.

I grew up with cats, not dogs. Cats are my kind of "people." I now had to face a deep fear based on three unrelated unpleasant experiences (dog bites). The unpleasant experiences only cemented my certainty that I was right to act this way. But luckily, a diversity learning experience, Obi, came into my life, and I listened and learned. The only reason that I changed my view of dogs was because I got to have an "emotionally, connected experience" with one. Prior to that, I had little exposure or experience with them, except three quite negative interactions.

The Obi Effect

This experience with a dog reminded me about how I have been on the receiving end of similar dynamics in my professional and even in my personal life. I have experienced judgments from people based on my dimensions of diversity without them even getting to know me. I have lived with unjustified behavior towards me driven by negative experiences others had with people who resembled me. Those were very painful and frustrating experiences for me. They often were never related to a personal/direct experience with me, but were based on stereotypes and unconscious biases about those with whom I shared similar dimensions of diversity. These same dynamics are an everyday reality for so many.

The way I often survived this type of treatment in my professional experiences was to focus intensely on the job I had to do. So, I tolerated the treatment and carried on . . . leaving those types of horrible situations as soon as I could. I know that many others use the same process to survive in these way too common instances, where DEI principles built on the Six Building Blocks have not occurred. It could have been, and can be, so much better.

Diversity training can be one of the best learning experiences of your personal and professional life. When we get up close and personal with authentic connections and have good trainers (facilitators), we can help shape people's preconceived notions. We can help people transform their own behavior to create a more inclusive environment and become better team members and leaders for people in all aspects of their lives. These are the types of life-changing experiences that well-designed and facilitated diversity, equity, and inclusion training support.

Organizational Development Theory in Practice

A VP of a large international organization felt frustrated. "Why do I still keep hearing complaints about diversity issues? We have held town halls and completed online training. People can even complete the training on their lunch break if they are too busy with work. I do not understand it," he stated. It is sad to think about how many times we have had this initial conversation with a potential client and/or heard about similar sentiments expressed to our DEI colleagues.

Organizational development theory has so much to offer diversity training initiatives because its practitioners know that an organization is composed of many moving parts. You need to address all the parts for successful long-term change. In diversity training, we talk about the Three-Tier Model. The Three-Tier Model describes a need for the focus to be on three levels to create long-term change and transformation:

Level One: Personal/Internal: Relates to one's personal beliefs, values, life experiences, biases, stereotypes, etc. It explores questions such as: What do I believe? What biases may I be holding? How have my life experiences impacted me?

Level Two: Interpersonal and Intergroup: Relates to how one interacts with others, including interactions between individuals and groups. Examples: How do men and women interact? How do new hires and long-term employees relate to each other? How do the sales teams interact with the marketing groups?

Level Three: Organizational Policies and Procedures: Relates to the organization's policies and procedures, as well as the written and unwritten behavioral norms. Examples: Do our recruitment and hiring policies and procedures support our DEI values? Do our compensation processes support equity and inclusion?

DEI training needs to touch on each of these areas to have the best chance of success. For example, someone may have a very strong personal value of equity in salary level and promotional opportunity, but if the compensation policy has strict rules about salary levels and standard requirements for promotional opportunities, the manager will not be able to make that happen. Or, there may be "rules" (unwritten) that no one gets to middle management without a college degree, or that three years of experience are mandatory for a promotional opportunity in another area.

It can be very frustrating and demoralizing when a dedicated manager attends a great DEI training session only to discover that the company's policies and procedures are stacked against the DEI future that was just discussed in the DEI training workshop. This can have disastrous effects all the way around the organization. Be diligent in making your DEI training inclusive of all three tiers of organizational change and the results will be brilliant!

Intention Does Not Equal Results

When many people think of diversity, they think of race, gender, and other forms of difference. We want to rebrand that notion so that people see the truth about diversity and the path to effectiveness with diversity. That path involves basic human connections and personal behavioral change. The workplace is an inherently diverse environment. That fact is the basis of DEI work. Our efforts should face that fact and promote learning that allows that fact to benefit everyone.

Diversity work *intends* to level the playing field. Instead, it often creates "us vs. them" distinctions. It *intends* to create inclusive workplaces. Instead, it deliberately excludes some people. DEI training *sets out* to empower (some) people. Instead, it engages in the one thing adults naturally rebel against—being told what to think.

We propose an approach to DEI efforts that allows all people to participate and addresses all their needs. It focuses on managing each individual as an individual and managing teams as a collective mix. We envision an environment in which people are comfortable and productive working with other people. That simple vision need not be clogged with unnecessary complexity.

Diversity and Exclusion

The promise of diversity management assumed that it would provide equal value for everyone. If it were done according to the original construct, there would be no difference in the benefit to large corporations versus small businesses, domestic versus international businesses, traditional (White male) workers versus nontraditional workers, and senior executives versus working-class people. Diversity management was designed to give us a reason to access talent in different packaging (familiar and unfamiliar), to make it profitable to assume that the contributions of all employees are worthy of consideration, to overcome the tendency to prefer some identities over others, and to allow everyone to participate so they can celebrate the accomplishments of a true team effort.

The temptation to reduce diversity management to a study of cohorts and dimensions of diversity has hurt the effort to create a discipline for the field. True diversity management is not a function of identity. A team comprising of all White men is just as much of interest to a diversity management practitioner as a team comprising several races, both genders, multiple functions, and several cultural orientations. The management discipline of diversity management is about managing to the individual rather than managing to any group identity. Dr. R. Roosevelt Thomas Jr.

pointed out that White men are just as odd (different) and just as normal (similar) as all other groups.

The same is true of all people. No one can be defined by a single dimension of diversity. In like manner, no two people share the same set of dimensions. Two Black men invariably have some things in common and they have some differences. The reliance on dimensions of diversity made it inevitable (given our social conditioning) that White men would be candidates for exclusion.

What About Bob?

(Jim) In 1996, I wrote an article for the *Managing Diversity Newsletter* entitled "What About Bob?" I warned that it would be a big mistake to exclude White, non-Hispanic, non-immigrant, able-bodied, heterosexual males from the diversity management conversation. I argued that White men (collectively) were unnecessarily being projected as the "enemy." This section of that article illustrates the problem we created by being selective in our inclusion.

> *"Inclusiveness cannot be redefined to exclude one group. In fact, failure to deliberately include White men in the debate, the strategy, and the implementation of diversity management will lead to its predictable failure. White men will respond to exclusion in natural human ways. They will band together; they will withdraw support; they will guard the old ways; they will get even. Making full use of our nation's human capital requires that we include all available talent and that we remove all barriers (including assumptions of privilege) to individual achievement."*

Now, as we look at the state of the movement, both inside major enterprises and in the larger society, that article was prescient. The mistake we made was misreading the reality of being White and male in the American workplace. Many assumed that the inherent privilege of being White and male was extended to and felt by all White men. We were distracted by the top 1% and concluded that the other 99% had equal standing at the top. Because White men occupied over 90% of the top positions in corporate America and controlled the bulk of the wealth in the nation, many thought that experience was shared by all White men. The reality is much more complex and nuanced.

In the formative stage of the movement, White men played a pivotal role in the development of the platforms on which diversity management rested. It is a real disservice to them that their seminal work and their voices have been muffled in the current environment. The evolution of the field has seen a decline in the presence and influence of White men (except White male CEOs).

The Rainbow Solution

According to recent surveys, over 90% of newly appointed chief diversity officers (CDOs) in the United States are People of Color. That continues to be a mistake we can ill afford to make. Jim reminds us that "Unless we all contribute to the successful fulfillment of the goals of diversity management, none of us will ever realize the promise of diversity management." We need all dimensions of diversity represented in all aspects of diversity to be the strongest we can be; all the diversity research would attest to this basic concept.

The reality is that something happens along the way, often in the form of ugly unconscious bias by many in the field and those in the position of hiring candidates to lead and/or consult in DEI. The statistic of over 90% of newly appointed CDOs being People of Color is driven by something very deep, perhaps unconscious, and way too often undiscussable by many. The reverse is also true, as People of Color are often assumed to be experts in DEI and face embarrassing situations when called upon for DEI solutions. One Black executive said, "I am an engineer, doctor, marketing specialist, sales manager, etc. I am not a DEI expert."

We truly are all in this together and need to learn about each other and to face organizational and social truths, no matter how unconscious and well-intended, that are having a negative impact on the field. For example, White women have been told in DEI leadership job interviews that they have all the skills, are outstanding, and would be an incredible help to the company, but if they hire a White person for the job, even a White woman, that the employees of color would "go nuts," and that it was better to have a less qualified Person of Color (with far less knowledge and experience in the field of DEI) than a White person who was clearly more qualified. When people of any color collude and support these types of decisions, it hurts the whole DEI movement.

Let's get smart and do it together!

Chapter 2

Begin with the End— Know Your Why

"Doing diversity because everyone else is doing it is not a wise choice. Acting on diversity as a reaction to social unrest is missing the point. Engaging in diversity efforts with no strategic intent is a waste of time and resources. Doing pretty much what everyone is doing will get you pretty much what everyone else is getting—mediocrity."

—Jim Rodgers

The popular phrase, "If you don't know where you are going you will probably end up somewhere else" too often describes where an organization lands if they have not established clear ongoing objectives for DEI training. Diversity training affects people's lives, survival, and futures. It can also affect corporate values regarding equity and corporate responsibility.

Ideally, the objectives would be derived from a DEI comprehensive organizational assessment. Base the objectives on what you want to accomplish regarding DEI in your organization in the short and long run—then deliver on them in the learning events. Make the objectives doable, clear, and meaningful. If you are not "all in" on accomplishing the objectives, do not start this process—nothing is more damaging to the future of DEI becoming a through thread woven into your organization than false promises and broken dreams. Be truthful, authentic, realistic, and inclusive in all the training objectives that you set. Set them as if your future depends on it.

"Begin with the end in mind."
—Stephen Covey
"Start with Why."
—Simon Sinek

Let's Stay and Do This

(Laura) It was day two of an introductory DEI training for the senior sales management team of an international corporation. The DEI session was positioned at the end of a week-long executive meeting. The group just happened to be comprised of all successful, high-performing, powerful men (50% White, 30% Black, 20% Latinx) representing sales districts across the United States. Two days of diversity training was probably not the first choice for some of these participants. But the salespeople were all team players, and it was mandatory, so they took it in stride.

Day one of our DEI training had set a good foundation of DEI knowledge. We made sure that we thoroughly covered Building Block 1: "Know Your Why." If you are going to ask executive salespeople for two days of their time, you had best be prepared to discuss why. The candid conversation created a degree of trust among participants as they engaged in deeper and more focused DEI conversations than they had ever experienced prior to the training workshop.

As we started day two, there was an unmistakable sense of tension within the group. We (the facilitators) were not sure where the tension was coming from. No one wanted to talk about it. Finally, a courageous Black man opened the conversation by saying,

"I am not at all sure that you White guys are opening up as much as we are. I get the sense that you are holding back and that you think that you can safely do that because if nothing changes, you are still all set. The system has worked and will continue to work for you. Why should you even be motivated to do anything?"

Without a moment's hesitation, one of the White men shot back, "The system has never worked for me, and I have not been holding anything back. In fact, I have actively participated all the way along." That icebreaker created an intimacy and depth of conversation within the group about the impact of DEI on their lives, the business, their families, and the future of society. The atmosphere in the room was so powerful that one by one, participants declared that this conversation was too important to leave, and they began rebooking their late Friday afternoon flights because they did not want to stop.

As one participant returned from rebooking his flight for the next day, another participant would leave to do the same. This process continued until all had committed to work late into the night and into Saturday morning to continue the dialogue about how diversity had impacted their lives and how it could benefit their company. That dialogue was valuable to them and way overdue. They had discovered their "why." This is the type of discovery and commitment that comes from the inside out. It is also the kind that lasts.

What They Discovered

The organization went on to make steady progress in DEI in the United States and internationally. In fact, one very visible sign was the previously undiscussable truth: CEOs always were picked from the United States, were college-educated White men in a heterosexual marriage, and at least six feet tall. It was possible that they were overlooking and underutilizing some talent based on a blind spot.

Within a few short years, the first CEO from Latin America was named and was not six feet tall. The organization still had a great deal of DEI work to do, but the impact of that breakthrough experience, as well as other ongoing DEI work, gave people hope and a belief that the company was committed, and that things were moving in a positive DEI direction. During the Covid-19 pandemic, the same company attributed its research teams' ability to work with innovation and speed to the diversity of its research teams and their ability to work collaboratively all around the world.

This is just one of many examples of how organizations have experienced ongoing individual, business, and societal success from DEI training where human connections are made in a trusting and safe environment, and where adults are encouraged to learn in the way they learn best.

Having Vital, Candid DEI Conversations

Several factors led to this candid conversation between races, ethnic groups, seniority, and other dimensions of diversity. These elements are rarely a part of organizational behavioral norms and are seldom addressed in DEI educational offerings.

These factors include:

1. Trust was built on day one by skilled facilitators who did not judge, welcomed all perspectives, set a tone of safety for all participants, and left "space" for the participants to do the work they needed to do and say the things they needed to say. This opened up the door for the deeper DEI conversation on day two.

2. All the salespeople were aware of how DEI was part of the organization's strategic business plan and how they needed to get on board and learn all they could if they were going to be successful in meeting those goals.

3. The content of the DEI training had been carefully designed to give participants an opportunity to authentically, honestly, and without fear of retaliation, address how the DEI concepts impacted their everyday work life and the DEI challenges that they were facing.

4. The organization made its intention about DEI clear. There was a real expectation for change from the top of the organization downward.

5. The training was tightly connected to specific organizational objectives and the specific tasks for which team members were responsible. Participants could easily see the relevance and value of the training. It also helped them apply the principles to their business goals more easily.

6. In the spirit of adult learning theory, we set up the parameters of the DEI workshop and allowed them to do their work. The DEI work that they were ready to do allowed them to push themselves further than we could have ever "lectured" them to go.

The result of all these elements was a strong awakening and breakthrough on some important and impactful DEI issues that had always been there but had remained "undiscussable" prior to this two-day DEI experience. The training goal was met, and the impact was substantial.

Take the Risk

These types of deeper DEI conversations need to be part of the through thread of DEI training that generates real change for individuals, businesses, and society. The only way to do this is to tell your truth and listen to others tell their truth. It can feel risky, but the consequences of doing nothing are far greater.

It is imperative that we have authentic and honest DEI conversations across races and within our own race. For example, it is equally important for Whites to talk about how they look at other Whites, often along ethnic, religious, and socio-economic factors, and how People of Color look at each other along lines of skin color and hair texture. To meet your DEI training objectives, you need to make every person's reporting of his or her DEI journey welcome, important, and a vital part of the DEI dialogue.

Follow the Data

Research has shown that the ability to attract and retain a diverse workforce has a positive correlation with the bottom line, and not doing so has a negative correlation. Yet the lack of careful attention, planning, resources, accountability, and focus on the goals and objectives of DEI training rarely gets the strategic business and developmental focus given to other top business initiatives.

A common business practice is often described as, "This is just the thorough, strategic and careful way we do business." That is, until it is applied to diversity, equity, and inclusion. Too many organizations have fallen short on giving their diversity training goals and DEI management the focus and attention that they deserve. The price that will be paid is the lack of diversity in your organization, and/or the underutilization of the diverse talent that is there.

Your Employees Are Watching: "My Dear Daughter, Do Not Apply Here"

A senior executive who was frustrated with the company's lack of genuine follow-through on publicly stated DEI initiatives stated, "From what I have seen, this company would not be a good place for a woman to start her career. I am advising my daughter not to apply here."

Have you ever heard this or something similar? It might have been in reference to a company not being "LGBTQIA+ friendly," or supportive of people with disabilities, or even what part of the country they are from. Perhaps you have also expressed similar sentiments that caution people about stepping into a work environment that you know may be detrimental to their career growth based on their dimensions of diversity. These do not represent inclusive behaviors that benefit individuals, business, or society. Quite the opposite.

How sad is that? Very sad with proven bottom-line implications documented in 21st-century research. *Diversity Wins*, the third report in McKinsey Consulting's series investigating the business case for diversity, "shows not only that the business case remains robust but also that the relationship between diversity on executive teams and the likelihood of financial outperformance has strengthened over time." McKinsey Consulting's research also showed that attracting and retaining a diverse workforce has a positive correlation with the bottom-line performance. Does it get any simpler than that?

Know Where You are Going—Then Go
Assess Where You Are

Ideally, the DEI training objectives for your organization would derive from a DEI comprehensive organizational assessment. That assessment should include both a diversity readiness study to determine prevailing attitudes about diversity, and a culture analysis to determine how the group will respond to proposed changes to behavioral norms.

Base the objectives on what you want to accomplish regarding DEI in your organization in the short and long run. Then deliver on them in the DEI learning events. Make the objectives doable, clear, and meaningful. Be truthful, authentic, realistic, and inclusive in all the training objectives that you set. Set them as if your success depends on it—because it very well might.

Define Terms for Common Understanding

The definition of diversity as put forth by the founders of the movement involved both differences and similarities. According to Dr. R. Roosevelt Thomas Jr., diversity is "the collective mix of differences and similarities." That definition creates the possibility of overcoming our natural tendency to create artificial barriers between peoples. Differences are easy to see and result in a quick reaction (in three seconds we make up a story). Similarities are always present but are harder to uncover (in ten minutes we can get to know one another).

Too often, diversity-related training is oriented around goals it could not possibly achieve. It is not possible to eliminate racism, sexism, or inequality in the workplace or in the broader society simply by exposing people to information about elements of difference.

DEI training that connects people in authentic dialogue exchange can be a very powerful tool in helping people learn how to enhance relationships and generously listen to diversity challenges. An expanded world view can generate a solid opportunity to identify behavioral and policy changes that support the principles, espoused values, and goals of a diversity change effort.

Commit or Quit

If you are not "all in" on accomplishing your stated diversity, equity, and inclusion goals and objectives, do not start this process. Nothing is more damaging to the future of DEI becoming a through thread woven into your organization than false promises and broken dreams. Failures in diversity, equity, and inclusion training can taint the reputation of this work in your organization for years to come.

Organizational legacy is a real thing, both inside and outside your organization, and the cost is real. Once an organization gets a bad reputation for failing to follow through on its DEI promises, the word will rapidly spread through cyberspace and other shared pools of meaning, including recruitment pools, college campuses, organization lunchrooms, conversations at Starbucks, and even dinner tables. It is very easy to talk about what you are going to do concerning DEI, but it takes a much deeper strategic conversation to actually accomplish the stated DEI goals. This is where so many DEI training efforts fall short.

Interest in DEI has risen and fallen, and organizations have made numerous efforts to refresh the field, primarily by changing the language and condensing the approach. DEI is a marginalized topic in many organizations. Thus, it is important that leaders understand the value of DEI to business success and the importance of corporate/organizational social responsibility. Diversity training needs to support both of those needs.

Pay Off or Retreat?

Being clear about your "why" (established through Building Block 1: "Know Your Why") and communicating it effectively can help avoid missteps. DEI training needs to be a place where people can safely and openly discuss and engage in honest and well-intentioned dialogue on their thoughts and feelings about the workplace. The energy for DEI involvement that this can spark in an organization can be phenomenal. The pushback can also be quite stunning!

Think about this. One organization announced a new management team. Out of thirty-five managers, there was one Black man, two White women, and thirty-two White men. The astonishing response from many in the organization was, "See, because of DEI, now women and minorities are getting all the jobs. I knew this would happen." Even when many colleagues tried to point out the faulty logic of that statement, the angry feelings remained, and the distorted perspective was still tightly held by some individuals. As the old adage says: "A man persuaded against his will is of the same opinion still."

Responses like these, based on perceptions that clearly do not match the reality of a situation, are an indication that leaders have failed to agree on and to articulate "why" DEI makes sense for their enterprise. It also represents a lack of clear communication of Building Block 2: "Know Your Strategy." Without clarity about the DEI strategy, people will make up their own "why" and "how" strategy. Even though the data clearly does not represent "women and minorities getting all the jobs," the feelings are real. We all need to do our job to make the DEI training and strategy work.

How will you deal with this? Will you step away and ignore it, or will it become a norm that when misperceptions and displaced anger arise, the situation will be addressed and discussed? Diversity training that generates real change has to prepare participants to have the type of conversations that will become a daily reality as individuals and the organization continue on the DEI path. It is inevitable and essential if the conversation is to be authentic and behavior adjusted appropriately.

Are You Up for It?

Diversity, equity, and inclusion work is rigorous, deeply personal, experience-based, and if done well, life-changing. There will be pushback. It will mean that things will change. Some of the norms that people are used to enjoying will go away. One of those norms is referring friends for a job even if that friend is less qualified. The deal is sealed because the perception of the "word" of the employee making the recommendation is always considered reliable. This behavior is a cancer to the spread of equity and inclusion.

Most people get their first job through someone that they know which statistically advantages those groups of people that are connected to the people that are already there. If we are going to talk about inclusion in our DEI training programs, then some not so inclusive unwritten rules and operating norms that are currently in place must be looked at differently. A more diversity-mature, informed perspective or diversity lens may necessitate many changes in the way things have been routinely done in the past.

In many cases, it will become painfully obvious to those who may have meant well, that their behavior in the past was less than positive and had an unfair impact on others. In fact, the reported impact of well-intended behavior may be quite different from every DEI concept that you thought you knew.

Defining Moments in DEI Advancement

There will be moments that are life-defining for individuals, businesses, and society. These moments raise questions such as: How committed are you? If you hold the power, how far are you willing to go? If you observe an injustice, or are told of one by a respected colleague, what will you do?

If you are on the receiving end of DEI missteps, microaggressions and/or oppression, how much are you willing to collude or tolerate? How much are you willing to change? These and other values-related questions and dilemmas will define who and what you are, and whether you are regarded as a champion and leader or as a complicit resister of diversity, equity, and inclusion.

Traps to Avoid

Do Not Litigate the Past

While conducting the executive interviews for a major large-scale change effort with a client company, the following dialogue occurred.

C-suite level operations officer (White male), nervously: "I must assume that you are here to help me and not to judge me."

Lead consultant (Black male): "I hope to show you that is the case."

This exchange illustrates that there is a narrative in existence that assumes a discussion of diversity-related topics with a White man is for the purpose of condemning or fixing, especially if the consultant is a woman or a Person of Color. Recognizing the fact that this dynamic exists makes it necessary for the woman or Person of Color to convince a person that they are not there to judge them, but to work with them and support the organization's DEI goals.

Skill the Future

It is important to keep the training focused on advancing DEI organizational goals rather than litigating the history of discrimination in America, and/or memorizing clever techniques of how to interact with those "other people." Some DEI training focuses exclusively on how to work with those "other people," including creating lists of suggested statements. This can bring a sense of relief and laughter to those looking for a script to use to interact with those different from themselves, and it might even be funny occasionally if it weren't so destructive to the advancement of diversity, equity, and inclusion. The understanding of how to manage the complexities of diversity, equity, and inclusion needs to be a much deeper and broader conversation.

It is not enough to teach people to respond by saying it was not their intention to offend. The conversation needs to discuss where those assumptions came from, the damage that it does to others and their careers, and their mental and physical health and well-being, not to mention empowering the vicious cycle of systemic racism. It is not enough to just know that is not your intent. To be effective, DEI facilitators must address the notion and offer a counter-narrative that confirms a more equitable and strategic intent.

The Right Endgame

The explicit objectives of some diversity-related training programs include rectifying inequalities, improving organizational climate and employee morale, increasing collaboration across lines of difference, fostering free exchange of ideas and information, and enhancing the hiring, retention, and promotion of diverse candidates. Diversity-related training should not be approached as something separate from helping people fulfill the general expectations of work life (working with others). It should be part of equipping people to succeed at their regular organizational duties.

We connect diversity-related training to skills and competencies, making them more likely to be retained and practiced. It is important to equip participants with practical tools and resources to identify natural human tendencies, and to recognize how these tendencies affect responses to diversity. This approach reduces the stigma, defensiveness and polarization associated with discussions of core dimensions of diversity.

Skills include relationship building and collaboration with diverse perspectives in order to advance organizational goals. The Six Building Blocks give us a template to reference as we implement DEI training based on the concepts that we've discussed. This will yield powerful and meaningful results focused on (a) human connection and behavioral change; b) sound adult learning theory; and c) organizational strategy and success.

Chapter 3

Connect DEI Training to All Aspects of Business Strategy

"Diversity is about all of us, and about us having to figure out how to walk through this world together." —Jacqueline Woodson

Strategy, by definition, is the position a company must hold to win. Part of any strategy is a people component—who we hire and how we manage them. Understanding human behavior is key to getting people to work together more productively. A portion of each training session should be dedicated to highlighting the organizational strategy that undergirds the need for diversity training. Just positioning the training as a response to strategy changes the dynamics of the session. It is more attractive to be "equipped," rather than to be "fixed."

Pain, Gain, or Strategy

Organizations adopt serious DEI efforts for one of three reasons: pain, gain, or strategy. Organizations in pain are usually suffering through some major disruption that calls into question how they have managed relationships with employees and/or customers. The goal in those cases is to relieve the pain. Companies seeking gain from diversity challenges will try to capitalize on the current trend. Those interested in authentic diversity initiatives will get busy integrating diversity, equity, and inclusion into every business challenge that they face.

Minimizing Pain

In the late nineties and early 2000s, companies such as Texaco, Coca-Cola, and Johnson & Johnson were dealing with high-profile discrimination lawsuits filed by their own employees. It was a temporary painful adventure that hurt their brand and made them get serious about diversity. That seriousness translated into a few high-profile PR moves and some serious internal moves. Diversity-related training was a component of the internal moves, but it only involved select lower-level employees, seldom the executive corps, and was not integrated into long-term business strategies.

Predictably, once the negative publicity was gone, the companies tended to lapse back to their former state. The companies engaged in some version of diversity training to demonstrate that they were responding to issues raised in the lawsuits, thus minimizing their pain. In those cases, legal concerns trumped the learning opportunity, potential individual growth, and business success.

Reaping the Gain

Organizations motivated by gain are opportunistic in their decision-making. When it is popular to do so, or when there is a public appetite for some grand gesture regarding race, gender, disabilities, generational acceptance, or other diversity-related causes, these organizations declare themselves diversity-friendly and make bold pronouncements to the public about their good intentions. They seldom focus any of that fervor on improving their internal capability with diversity.

This approach is always short-lived and will have to be repeated when there is a new societal catalyst. Its failure is evident by the lack of representation in the ranks of Fortune 500 CEOs. Richard Zweigenhaft, of *Diversity in the Power Elite*, reports that 2020 figures show that 92.6 percent of Fortune 500 CEOs self-identify as White, Non-Hispanic; 3.4 percent identify as Latinx; 2.4 percent identify as East Indian or South Asian; 1 percent identify as African American/Black; and 0.6 percent identify as Native American or other.

Strategy Is Sustainable

In the mid-2000s, PepsiCo adopted a strategy that focused on broadening its market reach. That diversity management strategy resulted in dozens of new products that appealed to new pockets of the snack food and beverage marketplace.

Procter & Gamble (P&G) was an early adopter of the diversity movement. But like so many organizations, they had tabled their effort as they tried to figure out how to use diversity management as a business tool. In 2000, when Alan G. Lafley became CEO of P&G, he decided to rely on the company's well-established capabilities with diversity management to revive and grow the company. He and the other senior executives reached back to the skills and perspectives they had learned in the early nineties under the tutelage of Merlin G. Pope Jr.

In *The Game-Changer*, a book that he coauthored, Lafley describes how they turned P&G into an innovation machine by relying on diversity as a strategic tool. The result was the launch of seventeen, billion-dollar products. Here are some of the principles P&G adopted with its diversity management strategy:

- Innovation is a strategy and a capability
- Fifty percent of innovations should come from outside P&G (inside/outside diversity)

- Intellectual diversity of teams (people with different ways of thinking) should be the norm.
- The whole point of a team is to take advantage of the potential of having diverse minds pointed to the same goal. The composition of the team itself is a leadership task.

The principle here is diversity (management). Game-changing innovation is achieved by harnessing diverse thinking and linking it with consumer insights. It also requires leaders to actively search for the right diversity of people. The generation and execution of these principles were strongly supported by human-connected DEI awareness work. That is the type of work that is needed for individual, business, and societal change to happen and endure.

On Business Strategy

Whenever a new chief diversity officer is announced, the statement says that he or she will be responsible for executing the company's diversity and inclusion strategy among other items. However, the statement never reveals what that DEI strategy consists of or why it is essential for the health of the enterprise. When you pull back the covers, you find that the so-called DEI strategy is really a set of operational plans and tactical activities. Nothing in the statement suggests the existence of corporate strategy.

According to Michael Porter (Harvard professor and author of *Competitive Strategy*), strategy is positioning. P&G's Lafley defined strategy as "a set of choices that position the firm in its industry so as to create sustainable (competitive) advantage and superior value." The key word is position. Strategy is about positioning your enterprise to win. In fact, it can be thought of as the answer to this question: "What position must we gain and maintain in the marketplace to win the competitive battle?"

It's also important to understand what strategy is not:

- Strategy is not vision. They are two different pieces of the essentials of enterprise planning that include mission, vision, values (as a surrogate for culture), and strategy.
- Strategy is not simply a plan. Operational plans and tactics are the ways you execute strategy, but they are not the strategy itself.
- Strategy is not whimsical. Once adopted, it should remain in place until the landscape of the industry marketplace changes so much that new positioning is necessary.
- Strategy is not best practices. Your strategy is unique to your business. No two enterprises can execute with the exact same tools. Doing what everyone else is doing will get you what everyone else is getting: mediocrity.

Origin of Strategy

This language of strategy comes from military science. For a military general, strategy is the position that must be achieved to accomplish the mission. For example, to win the battles in the Pacific during World War II, the US-led Allied forces had to control certain key islands. Those positions gave them the ability to see and predict enemy movements so that they were not surprised. That was their advantage and is why they won.

In like manner, companies must discover a unique position that gives them sustainable advantage against their competitors. In the case of DEI, it is not developing a DEI strategy, it is choosing DEI as a strategy. As a strategy, DEI can position a company with superior capability to use inevitable diversity as a value creator rather than as a distraction. Once organizations make the decision to adopt DEI as a strategy, plans can be made to ensure the effective execution of that strategy.

On Execution and Management

Equally important, if not more important than strategy, is execution. Once you establish that diversity management is how you will distinguish your company in the marketplace, you must determine how to make it a reality. The "how" of a diversity management strategy must follow and be in clear support of the "why." A tactical response to diversity without a clear connection to strategy rarely gets it right.

Target has been recognized for executing an effective strategy to compete against Walmart. Among the subtle elements of its strategy are the principles of diversity management, which are focused on customers, employees, and society. For example, in the company's DEI Corporate Report, Chief Diversity & Inclusion Officer and Senior Vice President of Human Resources Kiera Fernandez reports, "It's always been important to us that we build and develop a diverse Target team that reflects our guests and the communities we serve. Part of that commitment is setting data-driven goals and transparently holding ourselves accountable every day for making progress across the organization."

Interestingly, executing a diversity management strategy requires more skills at the frontline management level than at the senior leadership level. A DEI learning platform needs to include elements that develop managers with the motivation and skills to support the DEI strategy.

DEI Frontline Management Key to Success

(Jim) In my research of frontline managers practicing diversity management, I found that management perspectives and skills, much more than C-suite commitment, are the keys to effective execution of a diversity management strategy. Gallup research indicates that 80 percent of persons with the title and role of "manager" are not very effective in that role. Yet, they report that 70 percent of team effectiveness is directly tied to the manager. The frontline managers who are part of that top 20 percent seem to inherently understand and seamlessly practice diversity management as they work to achieve team goals and objectives.

Top performing managers accept that diversity management is a management discipline designed to get the best from all employees by recognizing the uniqueness of each person. They follow similar principles to get the best from a team composed of diverse employees. These principles include:

- Get to know them as individuals and at a deeper than normal level.
- Give them responsibility and let them shine
- Give them what they need to perform: encourage, develop, and support.
- Know yourself (and your triggers); don't allow your personal conditioning to get in the way of their development and growth.
- Listen more, talk less. Enough said.

Those same managers practice similar behaviors to get the best from teams of diverse composition. These behaviors include:

- Prefer diverse teams; avoid a team of yes-sayers.
- Manage conflict, tension, and discomfort; these factors are inevitable when broad perspectives congregate.
- Be a role model for diversity competency. Show them how to include and accept.
- Build team cohesion. Manage the collective mix for the benefit of goal achievement.

What's the Problem?

(Jim) At the opening session (Executive Education) for a new client, one of the junior executives asked, "What problem are we trying to fix (address) with this effort?" He may have thought I would be upset or feel challenged by his query. I could see the uneasiness his question engendered with the CEO and the CHRO. It surprised them when I said, "Thank you for that question. If you had not asked it, I was going to." I went on to explain that despite the social pressure and enlightened motives that brought us together, diversity management only matters to the extent that it helps solve a business problem. So, the first question should be, what is that problem? And, of course, it is important to have an answer.

In the case of ThyssenKrupp Elevator, it was ranked number one in market coverage (because of acquisitions), but last in market efficiency. The company suffered from a negative perception by a large portion of its relevant market because of its ownership and the makeup of its customer-facing employee group. It was hard and expensive for the company to service and maintain its acquired customer base. The company needed to develop a more diverse team of representatives and generate more creative ideas to upgrade its products. A diversity management strategy was an answer to that dilemma. The execution plan included diversity-related training for all employees.

Fact of Life

Diversity is a fact of life that must be considered as you manage the enterprise, but it's not the problem. You can't get good solutions by working on the wrong problem. So, if diversity is not the problem, what is? The only problem is that managers in most organizations are not conditioned, nor are they equipped, to manage diversity effectively.

Unfortunately, the discomfort, inconvenience, tensions, and distractions associated with diversity causes people to react in ways that create chaos, increase tension, and slow decision-making. Diversity management, not diversity, is our challenge. We have all had occasion to experience that nagging, uncomfortable feeling when interacting with another person or persons. We often cannot pinpoint what it is about that person that creates the feeling. We only know that the tension that ensues impedes our objectivity, blocks our ability to listen actively, and erodes our desire to collaborate.

The net result is we lose the opportunity to create a winning solution or quality decision based on the superior collective judgment that is available with diverse parties. The fact that we cannot pinpoint the real basis of the tension does not prevent us from assigning a reason. In the absence of good data to explain any event, the brain will make up a reason. In this case, the reason will probably have to do with race, gender, sexual orientation, physical ability, ethnicity, or age—the internal dimensions of diversity. Yet, our rational minds tell us that these traits are seldom the sole or major cause of diversity tension. They are simply convenient labels to use when real data eludes us. That is the impact of the dreaded "D" (diversity) word.

Research Support for DEI Strategy

Strategy can be supported by research findings. Walmart's strategy of being perceived as having the lowest price for every item it sells was based on extensive market research that showed there was a large population of consumers for whom price was the major factor in a buying decision. Positioning itself as the low-price option has paid off by making it number one in its market space.

The support for diversity as a strategy comes from groundbreaking research in complex problem solving by researchers like

Dr. Scott Page of University of Michigan and the Santa Fe Institute. Dr. Page outlined his findings in the book, *The Difference*. He did not set out to prove the efficacy of diversity management. Instead, he attempted to find how humans interact when faced with complex problems and obscure predictions. The diversity findings were a by-product of his research.

In his words, Dr. Page describes how and why diversity is a viable strategy for many enterprises:

> One of the things social scientists do is create math models to prove our theories. I constructed a formal model that showed mathematically that diversity can trump ability, and under what conditions it does. Our models are like what people are doing to predict the financial markets and voting patterns.

The model showed that diverse groups of problem solvers outperformed groups of the best problem solvers. The reason . . . "The diverse groups got stuck less often than the smart individuals, who tended to think alike and therefore get stuck at the same point. It also showed that the right perspective makes any problem easy."

Common Sense Strategy

Some things are just common sense. Most people believe that it is better to have access to a broad range of perspectives and to get the best from everyone on the team. The old adage "Two heads are better than one" is especially true when the two heads have differing points of view. But because we believe something doesn't mean we will act on it. The question of what gets in the way of following common sense logic can be summed up in one phrase: human nature. We need evidence to confirm our natural belief. We know that sometimes acting naturally can have unintended consequences.

But some logic can be confirmed through observation almost daily. Because of human nature, we develop a set of expectations and criteria for acceptance. They are called our preferences. We prefer some things and don't prefer others. A key principle of diversity management is that we learn to make decisions based on requirements rather than preferences.

The qualities, traits, and characteristics we prefer in others are a way of determining how comfortable we are with them. There is nothing wrong with being in your comfort zone. That is why we tend to have an affinity for those who look like us, think like us, work like us, and have the same values and beliefs we have. We sit together in the break room with people we are comfortable with. We "hang out" with those we feel are like us. But defaulting to what is comfortable rarely allows us to make the best choice.

Our personal biases are very subjective and hard to measure. They are hard to define. Yet, they can become the primary factors for the decisions we make about other people. It is easiest for us to see positive, desirable traits in people who are most like ourselves. It is more difficult to see them when they come "packaged differently" (different gender, accents, country of origin, perceived social class, sexual orientation, age, race, physical abilities, etc.). A key principle of diversity learning requires that we begin to recognize the "right stuff" (applicable skills, experience, potential, etc.) when it comes in packages unfamiliar to us. Otherwise, we can overlook the best person for the job or not see worth and value in others who are different from us.

Adopting a diversity management strategy based on common sense runs up against human nature. That is why diversity-related learning experiences must focus on overcoming human nature. It requires an experience that provides a human connection with those who are different from us to help us experience and recognize the impact of decisions borne of natural instincts. People tend to naturally embrace similarity and step back with caution, or not at all, towards differences.

How DEI Strategies Produced Value

Most organizations never realize the benefits of diversity management because they never intend to. However, those that have invested in DEI strategies see payoffs.

SymCare

SymCare is a medical service company that provides constant monitoring and maintenance of chronic diseases like diabetes. As a technical startup, diversity management was a key to its early successes. The initial management team was deliberately selected to be as diverse as possible. The relevant diversity included company insiders and outsiders, different functional expertise, different experience in global geographies and cultures, and different temperaments, as well as different ages, races, genders, sexual orientations.

Because of careful management of this diverse team, SymCare completed its compliance certification in eleven months, a process which normally takes twenty-six to thirty-six months. It saved the parent company millions of dollars in startup costs and eventually generated $12.5 million in revenue nearly two years ahead of schedule.

Consumer Vision Care

Johnson & Johnson Vision Care, Inc. (J&J) operated around the world, including in Japan, but sales in the country were lagging. The diversity officer for J&J suggested, against the advice of culture advisors, that they add more women to the sales force. The reason: over 50 percent of Japanese optometrists and ophthalmologists are female. The company implemented the suggestion and sales tripled. Japan became the number one market for Vision Care products.

Apple Computer

When the original MacBook design was unveiled, it had some obvious flaws. The original design team was not very diverse, mostly young, White male engineers with a clear American perspective. When the diversity officer saw the design, he challenged the team to go back and reconstruct the team using diversity management principles. The new team was more global, more ethnically diverse, more gender diverse, and more age diverse. The result is a multibillion-dollar product used by a broad range of people around the globe.

High Museum of Art in Atlanta, Georgia

The High Museum of Art was not growing in importance alongside the massive growth of its hometown of Atlanta. The leaders of the museum developed a comprehensive diversity management strategy that complemented its overall business strategy. The diversity management strategy was assigned to the chief operating officer and the chief financial officer. It was meticulously executed. The focus of the diversity management strategy was to broaden the appeal for membership growth and audience expansion. The result: membership reached all-time high levels and audience size for exhibitions more than doubled. The museum was eventually ranked in the top five of American art museums.

PepsiCo

PepsiCo had a long-standing commitment to diversity and diversity management. One of its many employee resource groups involved Latinos. The group suggested some new flavoring for Frito-Lay products, but their ideas were originally rejected because most of the employees were not in product development jobs. However, senior management intervened and got the products developed. First year sales of the new products exceeded $100 million.

These examples illustrate the argument for diversity management based on results, not rhetoric. Too often our basis for supporting diversity management is hope and aspiration. We support it because we believe it will produce higher performance. Yet, we seldom test that belief with real demonstrable effort. Those who have can safely promote the efficacy of diversity management by leading with results.

The role of diversity-related training is to help prepare individuals, managers, and leaders for the task of promoting the value of diversity management. It is a much easier and more sustainable sell when tied to strategy.

What Are We Doing Here?

There is often a fine line between doing DEI work for business success or for society and social change. We say what is good for your business can be good for society. In these days of heightened corporate social responsibility and social justice issues, the research shows that the dynamic of representing what organizations are doing in the corporate social responsibility and social justice arena is a very important factor for business success.

It affects the organization's ability to attract, recruit, and retain top talent and it even impacts the sales of products. It is not surprising that even companies that have a long history of discrimination cases and corporate social responsibility concerns now post inclusive messages regularly on their websites. Business analyst Jim Cramer once said, "All social change starts with business."

If business enterprises adopt a diversity management strategy, embrace the value-added approach to DEI, and practice diversity management at the team level, those principles can transfer into the larger society and a make a difference in how average citizens accept and appreciate each other. After all, most people share a common life practice. We all go to work somewhere.

Strategy: An Essential DEI Training Topic

To set the stage for a successful learning experience, it can be useful to establish why the event is happening. After the opening preparation for learning and after the housekeeping items are outlined, we suggest you ask participants, "Why are we here? Why has your company chosen to invest in this training for you?"

You can expect a range of responses to that question. The cynical members will refer to past shortcomings or current social unrest. Others may suggest it is the right thing to do. Often, some members have heard that there is a strategic rationale for the training. That is the time to have a short reveal of the company's strategy and how the content of the learning session supports that strategy.

It is best to state the context of the decision, the intent of the DEI learning session, and how it fits with other efforts relating to the diversity management strategy. The most important element of this short training sequence is the behavioral expectations associated with the new strategy. The strategy discussion helps members believe they will be equipped for success in the emerging corporate climate rather than them (the participants) being fixed. It relaxes the atmosphere and provides level ground for all the learners to participate—and it takes just fifteen minutes.

In many of the organizations that we have worked with, the CEO or a member of the executive team is always there to welcome people, share the training's relevance to company success, and share a personal story about his or her own diversity journey. They may use a personal story of how they or someone they love has been impacted. The topic is much less important than the vulnerability and authenticity. One CEO talked about his son's battle with dyslexia and how he had witnessed and felt helpless about the pain, frustration, and even bullying that his son had experienced, and how it had so devastatingly impacted his son's life. He declared that he was 100 percent committed to making sure that no one in the company would ever experience those feelings due to their differences. He said, "We are an inclusive company dedicated to everyone's success."

Stop the Criticism

During the recent social unrest in the United States, many companies have responded with bold statements in support of diversity and inclusion. This is a recurring pattern for organizations that seek to gain from an emphasis on diversity. Corporate leaders are being held to a new and different set of expectations by the public. Increasingly, they are held accountable for their values and the actions that accompany them.

While declarations, accompanied by a big check, can seem noble and can get a quick positive response, they rarely translate into real sustainable change. Look inside many of the organizations declaring themselves diversity-friendly and you will find scant evidence that they desire to practice diversity and inclusion for good commercial or social reasons. The fact that none of the so-called diversity targets involve deep learning or behavioral expectations of executives and employees is a clue that the efforts are intended for gain not improvement.

The preferred motivation for adopting a diversity initiative is strategy. This is when an executive team looks at the competitive landscape and concludes that there is advantage available by adding diversity management to their strategic mix. This is a deliberate decision based on good business intentions and not coerced by disruptive circumstances. Strategy is enduring. It takes time to produce benefit. It is seldom a topic of public discourse. After all, you don't want to give away the secret sauce.

Chapter 4

Adult Learning
People Hate Being Told How to Think

"Give a man a fish and you feed him for a day. Teach him how to fish and you feed him for a lifetime."

—Lao Tzu, Chinese philosopher

The two most important factors in achieving successful diversity and inclusion training are the facilitators and the design of the exercises. DEI facilitators must have the skills to effectively guide participants through exercises that involve honest and deep reflection of diversity issues by participants. Facilitators must be focused on the participants and keep all participants safe, whether they agree with their viewpoint or not.

A successful diversity training session must create an environment of "a type of meritocracy of pain" based on sound adult learning theory. What that means is that we all have pain around issues of difference, no one is exempt, and the sooner we use that mutual experience to bond and better understand each other, the more effective we can be in creating long-lasting behavioral change. Effective DEI facilitation requires an innate understanding of human nature and a set of skills that separate facilitation from training.

Adults Do Love to Discover Something New

Screams of denial, sidelong glances of questioning (and possibly some judgment), and squeals of laughter fill the room as participants engage in one of many frequently used exercises in DEI training. The process is quite simple and effective. Participants are given an index card, asked to hold it print-side down, and to not talk during the exercise so that everyone can have his or her own learning experience. They are instructed to turn the card over and silently count the number of Fs that they see on the card. Sometimes we will be even more explicit and reinforce the fact that "F" is the letter between the letters "E" and "G" in the alphabet. When they are done counting, they turn the card over. Then we ask them to congregate in groups based on the number of Fs they saw.

What is so fascinating for everyone, and mostly for the participants, is the phenomenon that occurs next. Without exception, participants vary on how many Fs they see on the card, and everyone believes they are right. Absolutely and unquestionably "right."

After we give them another chance to count, some people begin to change groups as they suddenly report seeing more Fs. We often hear judgmental comments about those who change groups and reflective comments about seeing different counts. Quite often we will allow a third count and even more people change counts and join different groups. In the end we reveal the number of Fs that are on the card. Still, some people refuse to believe and/or see them until someone is literally "in their face" pointing them out. That phenomenon is sometimes called a "perceived reality" in DEI terms. The participants all experience different perceived realities.

The Opportunity to Learn

This exercise could be just an interesting intellectual exercise for some, and possibly quite annoying for others. But we have their attention. Participants discover that their human brain some-times betrays them. They had an opportunity to learn and expe-rience this themselves, and, even better, in some cases, teach it to each other at the end of the exercise.

We invite conversation (always asking, not telling) about why some people look again at the card to recount and why others do not. Some said that once they come to a decision, they hold on to it unless someone can prove them wrong. Others said that once they saw so many of their respected colleagues in the oth-er group, they knew that they were missing something. Still oth-ers explained that English was their second languages so in their minds, they read the statement in their first language and that made it much easier to find the Fs. It was a unique and import-ant opportunity for them to reflect in their own way on the many concepts raised through diversity, equity, and inclusion training.

By extension, people reflect on who and what influences them in their daily lives at work and in their homes. They consider how diverse their "circle of influence" may be and what diverse per-spectives are absent/non-existent in their lives. For some, a ma-jor awakening occurs on a societal level about whose "voices" are missing from their state, country, or even on the global level.

Opportunity to Let Go

If the facilitators had used the typical "expert" training lecture model, we would have shared the learning points of the exer-cise. If we did, we would look smarter, but there would most like-ly have been resistance and defensiveness about their level of commitment and self-knowledge. Instead, we let people know up front that we recognize that they come in with knowledge and strengths, as well as challenges and weaknesses just like all of us, including the facilitators. We confirm that we are not there to judge or evaluate them. Rather, we are there to present a number of diverse opportunities to learn about themselves.

We invite them to take the opportunity to learn all they can about human nature through the exercises, self-reflection, asking tough questions of each other, taking risks, and practicing "talking to teach and listening to learn." As identified in Building Blocks 3 and 4: "Know Your Audience" and "Know How to Deliver." Adult learners tend to respond best to these types of guidelines, especially in DEI work. They often breathe a huge sigh of relief inside as their fears of being judged or of being wrong subside and they can focus on the job at hand.

The Great Equalizer

One of the most beneficial outcomes of using training exercises to help people learn is that an interactive learning experience can be "the great equalizer." For example, when you have diversity in the room (by job title, gender, age, work department, seniority, or any other dimension of diversity), participants begin to realize that perhaps they do not see everything that they thought they did and that there is value in diversity. They are often humbled by experiencing the universality of the human experience which helps them be more open to learning and hearing opinions that are different from their own.

At no point in this exercise did the facilitators tell or lecture the participants about what they should be seeing, thinking, or feeling. The DEI learning was generated by self-discovery and by learning from others. It was an inclusive and personal process. It began to set a foundation for DEI learning built on mutual respect and collaborative learning. This type of learning, based on collaboration and self-discovery, stays with adults. That is what we need for lifelong learning and personal growth concerning diversity, equity, and inclusion. This approach reinforces the fact that there is something to learn here today. It adds benefits to your life, your business, and your community/society. Best of all, everyone is included in the process.

The Theory in Practice

In this book, we use the word training as a convenience of language. Our preferred language is a "learning experience." The intent of our training goes beyond transferring information. We intend for people (adults) to learn.

In his classic book, *The Adult Learner*, Malcolm Knowles reminds us that "learning involves change." Learning shows up as a change in behavior, habits, knowledge, and attitudes. If adults are not moved enough to effect some change in the way they conduct their lives, it is not likely that learning has taken place.

Unlike young children who come to information sharing as "sponges," adults come to information sharing with already well-developed points of view, value systems, and knowledge. Any guide or leader of a learning experience must take that fact into account as they try to navigate the learning process.

A Work of Art

Two important factors in successful DEI training leave participants wanting to learn more—the quality of the facilitation and the design of the exercises. Achieving effective balance between these two elements is one of our personal measures of a successful training session.

Laura often uses the metaphor of creating an art sculpture, telling the group that "we may use a little bit of this, or that, and do a little bit of this, or that, and in the end, it becomes a beautiful solid piece of DEI work that we create together."

The Use of Models

Luckily, there are a variety of excellent models that DEI facilitators can use to generate rich DEI conversations. Used properly, these models can lead to deeper understanding and lasting behavioral change, such as recognizing "blind spots" (things that we just cannot recognize from our perspective) and discovering how you are influenced and conditioned by others.

These moments of awareness often follow the emotional path. Just when you thought the situation was hopeless, and/or perhaps you felt helpless about how to help someone recognize behavior that was not helpful or supportive, there is a breakthrough moment. In the best of cases, individuals will step into leadership roles and exhibit authentic behavior that they never had done before. This can feel miraculous and is worth all the hard work. Once a deeper awareness occurs, people rarely, if ever, go back to their previous level.

The secret of effective models is that they give people a way to talk about difficult issues and their connection to them in a way that is totally inclusive and does not blame anyone. The model helps prove that everyone is part of the conversation, and everyone has the same human processes.

We all are part of the problem, and we all need to be part of the solution. Otherwise, when power shifts, as it inevitably does in organizations and society, we are dangerously close to changing the players, but not the patterns. Offering learning tools that support discussion, learning from others, and self-discovery are so much more effective with adults than telling them what to do and how to act.

The Perception Assumption Model

(Laura) "I just know that we can do diversity work in a way that will be helpful to people and make them want to do even more because they realize that there is something to learn and that we are all in it together. Please, if there is ever an opportunity to design our own (internal) design and training team, I would like to be a part of it."

These were the sentiments I shared with my manager at a very successful high-tech pioneering firm. Never doubt the power of setting an intention. Great things can happen! Eventually I and two of my esteemed colleagues began the journey of developing a diversity training program for over 150,000 employees internationally.

The center piece of the diversity training was what I named the "Perception Assumption Model." In graduate school at Harvard University, I was challenged and inspired by the late Chris Argyris, one of my professors. Chris worked with Don Schon at MIT on a theory called "double-loop learning." A major part of their work dealt with what they called one's "espoused theory" (who you say you are), one's "theory-in-use" (what you actually do), and the gap between the two.

I immediately saw the connection of their theory to the behavior of so many of the well-intentioned managers and others that I was supporting as a senior human resource business partner. Especially in issues relating to diversity, equity, and inclusion, they would say one thing (espoused theory) and do another (theory-in-use). It is really hard to point that out to anyone, especially around DEI challenges. As a society, we have made only baby steps into that conversation.

I decided to create a model that people could use to analyze and learn about their own behavior. Hopefully, it would help people get a better understanding of their own and others' behaviors as part of a universal human process. I wanted to inspire and empower people to do more DEI work, not less; to have meaningful conversations that can be so awkward otherwise.

This model is based in part on my understanding of at least some of Argyris's and Schon's brilliant work along with my own research and interpretation. In many ways, my model became the vehicle for the adult participants in DEI training workshops to learn in a way that they would not have if they listened to a lecturer about their behavior or anyone else's. It also is a tool that people could share freely and joyously with others, such as their staff, co-workers, friends, and family members. It anchors diversity, equity, and inclusion work as something that is a global human phenomenon. We all share, contribute to, and are impacted by the human behavior represented in the model.

The Perception Assumption Model (Exhibit 1) is quite simple:

Exhibit 1: The Perception Assumption Model

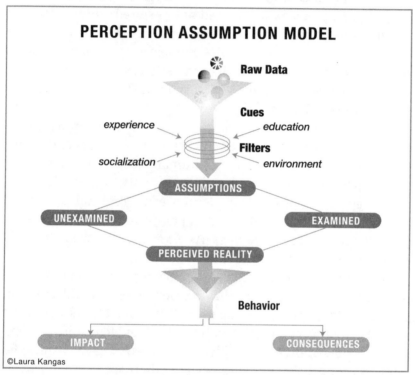

©Laura Kangas

Unpacking the Perception Assumption Model

The Perception Assumption Model represents a universal human process of being exposed to "raw data" which is the information we get bombarded with throughout our lifetimes. In fact, there is a fair amount of research that suggests that even when babies are in the womb they are taking in data! We often joke with folks and say, "So, if you are around anyone that is pregnant, be careful what you say because that baby is listening!"

Raw Data. Raw data is simply information that we are exposed to from a variety of sources. It comes to us through friends, family, teachers, ministers, media anchors, reading, and even our dreams. On its face, it is just data. It has no impact or meaning by itself.

Cues. Out of all that raw data, people pick up on different cues. Cues are things such as color, shape, and sound. Some people are more responsive and attuned to visual cues, others are more attentive to auditory cues, such as music or tone of voice, while others are more kinesthetic, so they are more impacted by touch, feel, and action. Cues provide context to the raw data so we can eventually make meaning of the data.

Filters. The next step is understanding that those cues, however we take them in, go through our own set of filters. Our filters are unique to each of us and include everything we have ever heard, seen, or experienced. They impact how we respond to the cues and make sense of them. Filters include everything you have ever been taught, read, and heard, including all the stereotypes and messages we have taken in, both consciously and unconsciously. They continue to be added to throughout our lifetime. It is quite startling for participants to recognize, through a series of interactive exercises, that most of what is in our filters is unconscious to us. However, it will impact our behavior if we are not aware of it, and even sometimes when we are aware of it.

Another important chilling dynamic of filters is that we do not even have to have a direct experience to create a message in our filters that can impact our behavior. We simply can hear about the people from that part of the city, or that work department, or that religious group, and left unexamined, you can begin to act as if it is true. That is how powerful messages in our filters can be.

Assumptions. Our behavior is impacted because our filters lead us to make assumptions. This is the point where we make meaning of the information we have been exposed to. Assumptions translate in our brains, not as a notion or possibility. They often show up as fully formed facts. We believe our assumptions.

Most of the time our assumptions go unexamined as though they were the truth. We do have the option of examining our assumptions. It takes discipline and is not our usual default. The benefits of examining assumptions is a key learning point in our DEI work. Whether our assumptions are accurate or not, they will generate our "perceived reality."

Perceived Reality. Our perceived reality is what we believe to be real and true based on our assumptions (which are driven by our filters). What participants soon begin to realize, or have reaffirmed, is that oftentimes our perceived reality may be quite different from reality, and often quite different from someone else's perceived reality. For example, two people can be sitting in the same meeting and experience it quite differently, based on their own perceived reality.

Behavior. What is alarmingly universal is that whatever our perceived reality is, whether it is accurate or not, it will drive our behavior. What we know about behavior is that it has both short-term impact and a longer-term consequence. These short- and longer-term impacts and consequences impact people's careers, lives, business, and society.

Impact and Consequences. This is the level of the process that most affects others. How we treat others impacts people's lives. Once we have said something or done something, it is no longer just our problem. It affects other people and creates a basis for others to assume things about them and behave according to those assumptions.

Time Lapse. With so many steps, you would think that this process may take a few seconds to play out. The fact is that it occurs in a few nanoseconds. We can go from exposure to raw data to some form of behavior without much time in between. We need to be aware enough of the process to disrupt it before damage is done.

In his insightful book, *Triggers*, Marshall Goldsmith reminds us that in our quest to be the good person we say we want to be, we have to be alert to those things that trigger us into avoiding behavioral change. The Perception Assumption Model illustrates how those triggers are formed and how to take steps to manage them.

Why It Works

There are seven things that make the Perception Assumption Model so effective and powerful in DEI training:

1. It is inclusive. The fact is that all people are included in this human process: all races, genders, sexual orientation, and all other dimensions of diversity.

2. It offers an explanation of how we arrive at the assumptions that we make about others.

3. It offers an explanation and better understanding of why people make missteps in DEI, and how it is often not a result of malicious intent.

4. It recognizes the limitations of anyone trying to "get better" at DEI without engaging with those who represent diversity to them. Without diverse input into your own filter system, it is very difficult to impossible to expand your filters to gain DEI information that would be significant enough to change your behavior.

5. It offers a way to learn. By seeking to increase messages and information about DEI, combined with a deep commitment to examining your assumptions, you have a chance of increasing your awareness and impacting your behavior.

6. It makes it clear that this process is universal and happens to everyone. Everyone needs to own his or her own part and work on it together. We can never solve it by working in a vacuum or by blaming one group.

7. It gives proof and hope that we can be better. It may not be easy, and it might be embarrassing, but it will facilitate change and can change the world.

The Joy of Learning

How different it is when you give people a model, let them tell their story, share their individual challenges and strengths, and help each other learn about DEI. This model is just one of many to help facilitate DEI dialogue using the best of adult learning theory.

Experiencing Similarities

We have always defined the word "diversity" as including both differences and similarities. Based on science, research, and observation, we are convinced that any group or pair of humans have more in common than not. The differences are often more obvious and certainly more talked about than the similarities.

Part of the exciting possibilities that arise from effective diversity-related training based on principles of adult learning is discovering how similar we all are. We, of course, could teach people the science and the logic of that reality; however, the alternative and more effective method is to let them discover and experience the similarities themselves.

The Wisdom Approach

Our experience and the wisdom of the ages teaches us that we overcome darkness with light; we overcome hate with love; we overcome ignorance with knowledge. It does little good to focus relentlessly on the thing you want to change. It is more valuable to promote the thing you want to become.

In that spirit, we propose that we cannot overcome our natural reactions to otherness by focusing relentlessly on what makes people different. Differences are very important and need to be discussed and understood. Our similarities are also important, and we can learn to spend time to find out what we have in common.

Differences often trigger us to be wary unless we have done serious DEI work to understand their inherent value, and then it still can happen (on an unconscious level). Similarities can prompt us to draw closer so we can build the trust needed to have authentic dialogue about our differences.

Exploring Similarities through Differences

In our learning sessions, we use adult learning tools like self-reflection to invite participants to rediscover who they are beyond their titles. For example, one exercise asks people to list attributes about their life such as place of birth, ethnic origin (or bloodline), early life experiences, family structure, breadth of travel, education (formal and informal), key values, and others. We then ask them to share their list with a small group of cohort members with instructions to notice the differences. We (DEI facilitators) notice that after sharing, spontaneous conversations break out at the table groups, which we allow to continue for a few minutes.

The debrief often goes like this:

Q: What were some of your observations about your fellow participants? What did you notice?

A: We noticed how different our life paths have been. For instance, I discovered that Bob had traveled to all fifty states and that Shaniqua was born in France and had studied in Mexico.

Q: We noticed that after reading your lists, you started talking to each other. What was that about?

A: (Invariably, some version of this response will arise): Well, you asked us to notice differences, but I was struck by how much we had in common. For instance, Jerry and I have worked together for five years, and I never knew we came from the same small town. I thought I was the only one with a Greek bloodline, but I discovered that Mary and I are probably related. John hunts in the same reserve I hunted in with my father. And the list goes on.

Participants are offered an opportunity to genuinely experience human connection with people they knew, but until the DEI training, they never realized that they had a connection to, especially in such an important way. These are powerful experiences, and many participants report that people even begin to look physically different. They notice things they never saw before and feel a connection that prior to those moments during the DEI exercises, was never felt. Years of business and team productivity continues to tell us how these types of deep connections lead to team loyalty and outstanding commitment to the team's and organization's success. Everyone "wins."

Language versus Practice

DEI is just the latest iteration of the language roulette we play to label the variety of activities and principles we call diversity. Instead of advancing the field, many have found it more convenient to change the language. For us, advancing the field involves finding better ways to execute what we already know. It does not involve adding new exotic sounding concepts to the field.

Diversity training started as a component of workplace diversity, as opposed to social, political, academic, or cultural constructs. In the workplace, DEI should be concerned with creating more comfort and productivity among team members through relationship building, better human connection, and changes in personal behavior. It is a simple objective and a simple process. It has fallen victim to the natural group process of over complication. To fulfill Building Block 6: "Know How to Deliver," we recommend using solid adult learning fundamentals as the foundation of all your DEI training.

The Basics

World class DEI facilitators tend to focus on the basics. Introducing people to doctoral level concepts like anti-racism, unconscious bias, critical race theory, oppression, cultural divisions, or pluralism only prove how smart the facilitator is. While these concepts are important to the evolution of humankind, they are mostly for the intellectually curious.

The objective of DEI training is to help people build stronger relationships and figure out better ways to work with and create success with other people. These events address basics such as bias, prejudice, and reactions to differences (behaving on assumptions not facts). The objective of experiencing the basics is to learn to manage and control the impact of these human conditions. You can do this!

Chapter 5

Creating Safe Space

"People fail to get along because they fear each other; they fear each other because they don't know each other; they don't know each other because they have not communicated with each other."

—Dr. Martin Luther King Jr., Civil Rights Leader and Nobel Peace Prize Laureate

"We were all born into this. No one in this room created this. Our job is to try to understand it and move forward to make it a better world for everyone."

—Paul S. Bracy
Founder, Dock C. Bracy Center, Inc. for Human Reconciliation

If you move into the world of "shame and blame" in DEI training, you have lost sight of your goals and stand a 100 percent chance of not reaching them. People (adults) live in a world where they are already facing shame, stigma, social discord, and confusion. Understanding that "we were all born into this" is a phrase often used to refocus the group on the present moment and what we can control moving forward. The history and the pain is important to hear and understand, but we do not want to get stuck there.

Delivering DEI facilitation with a "Zen lens" requires moving from the familiar mindset of the trainer to the Zen (the practice of seeking the truth) of facilitation. If participants feel like the facilitators are pushing their own agenda and beliefs on the group—the training is doomed. These are the sacred responsibilities of DEI facilitators.

Generating Real Change through Facilitation

Do Not Ask Us to Go Again

"We love you as our HR consultant, Laura, but please do not make me go to one of those diversity workshops again. I felt judged, disrespected, and no one was listening to each other. I felt like the facilitators had their own agenda and it just made things worse. I am done." This diversity training experience clearly did not meet the message of Building Block 4: "Know How to Deliver." Diversity, equity, and inclusion work was in its developing stage in the corporate world, and I could see a great deal of good in the DEI-related workshops we were sponsoring. I also could see a lot of missteps with good intentions, and some missteps with less than positive intentions.

What I did learn unequivocally was that the DEI work would not move forward to meet its intended goals for individuals and the organization unless everyone was given an equal chance to participate in the diversity conversation, was sincerely listened to, and was treated with equal respect. People needed to see that these were the operating norms for the group. It was also abundantly clear to me that it was the workshop facilitators' job and responsibility to make sure that happened.

Face the Facts

The reality is that in this world there is a great deal of unacknowledged prejudice, discrimination, and injustices, perceived and real, that need to surface in successful DEI training. It is essential, however, that the facilitators manage this dynamic and not get caught up in it themselves. It can be emotional for the participants and facilitators to hear people's pain and experiences regarding DEI issues, and when it happens, it is not always easy to hear.

The role of the facilitator must be to support the safety of group members and to help everyone grow. It is not to work the facilitator's own issues out or take advantage of their role as a facilitator to bully group members who push the facilitator's "hot buttons." It can happen quite easily, and the result is never good.

A hot button is something that is an emotional issue for you, most likely because you have been on the receiving end of a hurtful behavior related to it. It can also be something concerning DEI that you have tried to explain to no avail, and your frustration level is at its maximum level because people do not understand you and are not changing their behavior or even acknowledging your truth. A DEI facilitator's job in training is to help people identify and acknowledge their hot buttons, and to help them and the group better understand and work through them. However, the ultimate job of keeping people safe can easily be lost if facilitators start working their own issues/hot buttons. Remember, DEI facilitators are human too, and it can happen at the most unexpected times.

Don't Get Hooked

(Laura) I was co-facilitating a DEI two-day workshop early in my career in New York at a big, well-known organization with one of my mentors, who also happened to be my boss. She's African American and I am White. Our group was primarily White men who clearly were in control in the company, held all the key jobs and high-level management positions, and were complaining about how women and minorities (as they described People of

Color) were getting all the jobs even though they were not qualified, how hard they (the men) had worked for their positions, and why others (women and People of Color) weren't just doing the same?

Having lived a life full of discriminatory actions based on my gender as a woman, I decided I had heard enough. (Note to self: this is not a good place to be for a facilitator whose job it is to keep the group safe.) To use another DEI facilitator "insider" term: I "went off" on them.

My hot button exploded into a tirade of telling them (yes, telling, rather than inquiring) that I was deeply offended by their attitudes and lack of understanding. I followed it up with what was supposed to be a question, but everyone knew it was the farthest thing from a question. I posed the statement/question to them, "Would you even have had a chance at the job you have now, and have had in the past, if you were a woman? Would you have been taken as seriously? Would you have had the connections that helped get you here? Let's not forget to consider if you were a Person of Color in addition to being a woman? (with an eye to my manager). My guess is that the story would have been much different, or at least much more difficult, if you were even given a chance to compete." The silence was deafening.

Luckily it was close to the end of day one, and we were able to dismiss the group and tell them to have a good evening, and that we would pick this up again tomorrow. Having said all that, I quickly realized that I was not at my best DEI facilitator mode in those closing moments, and I knew that I would apologize to the group tomorrow and use it as a learning experience and teaching moment to better understand how deeply DEI impacts people, their co-workers, their business, and society.

My Kaizen Moment

To my manager's credit, she coached me by saying, "Laura, you were lucky those were such nice men because you really went off on them." Her next words have deeply impacted how I facilitate DEI groups now, and I feel very blessed to have heard them that day. She said, "Your job is to keep participants safe and help them grow. One of your biggest challenges will be to understand that what you see as a "baby step" in DEI work for someone, could be a giant step for them. If we shut it down, and do not honor it, they may never take a step again and be able to grow."

That was a moment of continuous improvement (Kaizen) that has informed my facilitation work ever since. It illustrates why facilitators give each other real-time performance feedback. It is sometimes easy to get hooked. It is never okay.

Distinction between Training and Facilitation

The *"Zen of Facilitation"*, an article by Joellen Killion and Lynn Simmons, was published in 1992. It serves as the basis for much of the modern facilitation movement. At the beginning of all the TOF (training of facilitators) we conduct, this article is introduced as required reading. The effectiveness of a diversity learning experience relies on these principles of facilitation.

The Core Principles

1. *Facilitation involves moving from the known to the unknown.*
   a. The facilitator creates a nurturing environment for individuals to learn whatever they are comfortable learning.
   b. Remember that you are facilitating another person's (learning) process. It is not your process. Do not intrude. Do not control. Do not force your own needs and insights into the foreground.
2. *Facilitators trust their intuition.*
   a. Facilitators operate not so much from knowledge of "how to," but from "gut feelings."

b.   Stay in the here and now. The facilitator needs to stay in the present in order to focus clearly on what is occurring in the group. The past and future do not exist for the facilitator. The only information or interaction that matters is what is current.

3.   *Asking questions and listening are the primary functions of an effective facilitator.*

a.   These functions replace giving answers, assuming the group's needs, or providing solutions.

b.   "We are not here to answer your questions, but to question your answers."

The Facilitation Mindset

We have discovered that a facilitation mindset is essential to effective DEI training. It requires one to be willing to let go of his or her own needs and attend to the needs of others. It requires tremendous dedication to the concept of practice and reflection. It is not learned quickly. Being a pretty good trainer is not an automatic determinant of being a good facilitator. It is as much a mindset as a skillset. That mindset relies on a set of beliefs about people and their capacity to learn what they need to learn.

Belief 1: Facilitators trust the group's ability to find its own direction and resolution.

Belief 2: Creating a sense of community creates a forum for effective group work.

Belief 3: The facilitator needs to manage any preconceived notions.

Community is defined as a group of people who have learned to communicate honestly with each other, go deeper than the masks of composure, and to develop a significant commitment to rejoice together and make others' conditions our own. A facilitator believes that the group (community) establishes its own purpose and is capable of achieving its own outcome. In every situation, the facilitator believes the solution is possible any time before, during, or after an event.

The facilitator assumes the group's perspective rather than maintaining his or her own. Facilitators give up the need to be right or to heal, convert, solve, or fix the group. Facilitators take a backseat to the process and allow the group to drive itself. This behavior is antithetical to the trainer's role of directing the group toward specific outcomes.

Model the Behavior

When the facilitator models the productive behaviors of respectful listening, maintaining personal safety, honoring various perspectives, sharing, trusting, risk-taking, and disclosing, then group members will mirror these behaviors. As one masterful facilitator observed, "My best work is done when I forget my own point of view."

Zen is the practice of seeking the truth. The Zen of facilitation is not a religious practice, but rather a strong set of beliefs that drives our choices and actions and urges us toward discovering the "truth" through reflection. Thoughtful, mindful facilitators have to be deliberate in letting go of what they know, trusting the process of learning, suspending judgement of other points of view, and being vulnerable. Zen facilitators must go beyond knowledge and strategies to seek the truth and enlightenment that come only from practice, reflection, and following their beliefs.

Humble Inquiry

In his book, *Humble Inquiry*, Edgar Schein introduces us to the fine art of asking questions to which we do not already know the answer, and building relationships based on curiosity and interest in the other person. He goes on to say that humble inquiry runs counter to our culture, which overvalues telling. Skilled facilitators must learn to override that cultural conditioning and adopt a posture of service.

DEI facilitators must be focused on the participants and keep all participants safe, whether they agree with their viewpoint or not. This Zen style of facilitation is much easier said than done, but it can be cultivated by anyone deeply committed to helping themselves and others learn about DEI. It does require that facilitators become comfortable with not being the "expert" who is filling participants' minds with their own version of DEI wisdom.

To gain these skills, it takes a humble attitude, a willingness to study and practice, a willingness to listen to feedback and try again, and an understanding and commitment to DEI work. DEI work may be the most challenging and unique facilitation and lifelong learning experience that they will ever engage in.

Like a Jazz Concert

Facilitators are not crusaders. They follow the energy in the classroom and guide productive conversations. It is vitally important for us to consider ourselves servants and guides to DEI learning for participants. We need to meet them where they are and move with them wherever they need to go for their own learning. Laura's colleague, Dr. Thomas Gordon, guided her early on to facilitate DEI workshops "like a jazz concert," letting the group guide their own learning and to go with them where they needed to go. This is a sacred responsibility of DEI facilitators and one that helps create learning experiences that our participants will never forget.

Responding to Language Sensitivity

In the classroom, you will encounter different levels of language sensitivity. Some people get triggered and offended by the use of certain words. An example often raised in workshops is the use of the term "guys" to address all female and/or mixed-gender groups. Without human connected DEI training, this topic probably never gets discussed, unless it is in private conversations among the women in the women's bathroom.

When it has been raised, we often share the research findings explaining that masculine words functioning as neutral terms are expressions of a misogynistic social order. There is always a large amount of pushback. Many men become defensive, and some women even loudly proclaim, in solidarity with the men (or possible fear of retaliation), "Oh, it does not bother me!"

In the spirit of discovery versus lecture, we suggest that if words and language are not such a "big deal," and if we think women are being overly sensitive, let's use the term "gals" to refer to the entire group, at least until the end of the day. This is fun for about the first fifteen minutes. Then the somewhat condescending looks of annoyance settle in, which transition into anger, impatience, and frustration. The important DEI conversation can then begin about how people feel in this moment, and how similar examples apply to their professional work-life experience.

The *Washington Post* referred to the process like this: "The battle over language is a battle over belonging, and over who gets to define boundaries and limits." . . . "It's about expanding language instead of shutting it down and understanding that one person's experience of censorship is another's experience of social justice."

Intent–Impact Model

This encounter with language sensitivity is an opportunity to introduce a useful tool called the intent-impact model. Intent-impact is a way to examine the impact of things you say with no malicious intent. It is also a way for you to assert the impact of what others say without assuming malicious intent. Many vigorously argue that they do not mean any harm by their use of certain language. They add that, "It is a term I use with everyone." Some even go as far as to tell people how they should feel, using phrases like, "You are way too sensitive, just ignore it."

DEI facilitators need to guide this conversation to be a gateway to deeper conversations about what really matters to the people in the room and what words, actions, and/or treatment they can relate to about their identity/dimensions of diversity, rather than a battle of wills and power, which it so often is.

We can invite people to consider options like, "You can assert impact by saying, 'When you use that language, I feel like you don't value my point of view. Is that what you intended?' You can assert intent by saying, "When I use that word, I just want to simplify the language for ease of understanding. Is that how you hear it?'" The result is clarity of intent and an opportunity to determine impact. DEI training is a good place to discover and practice these skills designed to enhance DEI dialogue and potential learning, rather than cut it off.

Being aware of the impact of certain language on individuals may cause a perpetrator to rethink or discontinue use of that language in the presence of a particular person. That's a good outcome. It may also cause the perpetrator to double down and assert his or her own right to use the language. That is also a good outcome. At least then, you know who you are dealing with.

Head, Heart, and Hands Connected to Business Success

The Boston Consulting Group's holistic model for transformation includes the use of "Head, Heart, and Hands." It is important to include all three of these in DEI training. To be successful in this work, one must develop a true understanding of how DEI is critically important to organizational and individual business success (head); must make a personal connection with the ethics, values, and impact on individual lives (heart); and develop knowledge and commitment to taking action (hands). Too many of the standard DEI programs fall short of this because it is time-consuming and difficult work. Too often people want a script to read or a "silver bullet" (shortcut to making everything right), and too often it is falsely given to them in the form of DEI training.

Creating a Facilitated Learning Experience

Everyone needs to get foundational training, and managers need specific training on how to practice diversity management. We are changing behavioral norms, not just memorizing politically correct phrases and terms. Combining hard skills and soft skills in training is a delicate balance. Soft skills are hard skills in a workplace with diverse composition. Our ability to produce more widgets and create the next generation of widgets, is largely dependent on our ability to work productively with all our teammates. There are many training tools (multimodal) that can be used to facilitate the development of the "softer skills," but the DEI training designer must also have access to the key elements of the company's strategies, values, and business model to tie the training to those targets.

Materials and Process Need to Be Bias-Free

Facilitator materials need to be bias-free, inclusive, and easily applicable to real life in DEI training sessions. A common mistake of well-intended DEI training is that race and gender are addressed exclusive of other dimensions of diversity. The conversation needs to be about all dimensions of diversity. For example, in organizational life, it is important to discuss how People of Color stereotype White people, as well as how White people stereotype People of Color, to explore how men interact with women and how women interact with men, and how people entering the workforce look at those already there and vice-versa.

Facilitator Self Work

DEI faculty need to start with the exploration of the self. Potential facilitators must ask themselves, among other questions, "What don't I know that I don't know (unconscious incompetence)? What type of differences would be most challenging for me to handle in a training workshop?"

It is virtually impossible for anyone to lead a diversity-related training session before they are personally committed to a fair and impartial treatment of diversity, inclusion, and equity. That means that all people are on an equal footing.

The social corollary is this. Since the word "diversity" carries the baggage of assumed bias against Whites, males, straights, and right-leaning citizens, proponents of DEI cannot content themselves in knowing that they have inclusive intent. They must be blatantly overt in pronouncing and demonstrating that level of equity. For White people who feel threatened by the browning of America, they need to hear minorities declare, "We are not trying to replace you. We want to join you in continuing to build the house of abundance."

For advocates and practitioners of DEI, it is necessary to demonstrate that you are in it to help and not to judge. You have to lead people to a more equitable conception of DEI. As Dr. Martin Luther King Jr. once said, "You can't teach what you don't know. You can't lead where you won't go."

Superior Preparation Generates Superior Delivery

In the opening statement of a Train-the-Trainer session involving over sixty facilitators in preparation for a large-scale change effort, Jim said:

> What we are doing here is holy work. This material can be quite challenging for some people. Your role as facilitator is to lead with love. Don't judge (condemn) anyone's point of view. Let their classroom experience do the teaching. Allow them to do their own personal work and make their own choices about what knowledge they will embrace.

The people in the room were all seasoned, skilled, superior facilitators who had worked on multiple diversity-related training projects. They probably could have read through the training material and delivered a very good session without preparation. Instead, we exposed them to a training philosophy; we introduced them to the client company and its unique culture; we gave them strategic context for the project; we encouraged them to use continuous improvement practices (like the TQM concept kaizen) with their training partners; we asked them to treat this as a special case. Superior facilitators always prepare themselves to provide superior facilitation.

The point is when you do your best work as a DEI facilitator, participants often experience a range of emotions. DEI facilitators who practice what we refer to as the "Zen-style of facilitation" need to compassionately help participants learn skills to continue lifelong learning about themselves and diversity-related issues and concepts. This includes processes like inviting them to "notice what they notice" even when the workshop is over, and the facilitator is no longer present.

Sometimes that will bring up many negative emotions that were always there, but people never allowed themselves to express. We ask them to consider that it is good news that tough issues and questions are surfacing. "Congratulate yourself on making solid progress in talking about what is real so you can now be in the business of making it better."

Chapter 6

Engage Your Audience

"I am always ready to learn although I do not always like being taught."

—Winston Churchill

According to one recent study, people remember 10 percent of what they read, 20 percent of what they hear, 30 percent of what they see, 50 percent of what they see and hear, 70 percent of what they say, and 90 percent of what they do and speak. That is why we recommend experiential learning as the primary delivery modality for sensitive training like diversity-related training.

Experiential training is based on forcing participants to consider their natural response to other people and other situations. We invite them to consider new thinking because it is important to them, rather than instructing them on ideas that are important to us. The process of Experience—Discovery—Implication—Application is not just a classroom learning model. It is a life-learning model.

Experience, Discovery, Implication and Application=Sustainable DEI Learning

(Laura) "Were you my leader?" "No, I was not!" "Were you my leader?" "No, I was not!" The Trust Walk exercise was one of the many exercises we were using to engage the learners through a thought-provoking experience in our DEI two-day training retreat. Each Trust Walk consisted of a ten-minute journey of a blindfolded follower led by a leader. Each Trust Walk represented the diversity of each leader, some "introducing" his or her blindfolded follower to other followers and leaders, with some giving his or her followers sensual experiences like smelling flowers or touching ice. Some leaders opted for a much more quiet and almost meditative experience.

The final part of the exercise involved followers being instructed to draw a picture of their leader, whom they were soon going to have to identify to give them their picture.

The pattern of "Were you my leader?" continued around the diverse training circle as followers desperately tried to identify their leaders, quite convinced that their perception of their leader was correct. In my case (Laura and her follower named Barron), Barron continued around the circle until there was no option left but me: a 5'4" White woman of medium athletic build and one of two DEI facilitators for the session. The incredulous look on the 6'5", strong, athletic Black man's face was precious, and the impact of his courage to share his truth at that moment created a powerful learning opportunity for everyone: "I never would have believed that a White woman could lead me around, especially with a blindfold, and keep me safe. This is very powerful awareness for me. I have to think about how this plays out in my life."

Discoveries and Implications

Others quickly agreed that they, like Barron, realized that they had messages/stereotypes about others that impact their behavior and play out, often unconsciously, in choices about who and what they expect from people, and who they even feel that they can, or should, trust.

Application

But that was just the start, as participants realized it was not just about the question of expectations (though that was huge within itself), but also, who do they give prize assignments to? Who do they think is a "good fit" for the department? Who do they listen to more closely? What does this mean about them as managers, colleagues, and people? They realized the enormity of the roles that they played at the company and what if, just what if, they were heavily influenced by unconscious bias? This was the success of the company and people's careers and lives impacted at the end of all this . . . the application of the learning was clear as day to them!

Discovering the Gap

It was stunning and fun to see participants walk with great confidence and surety up to someone in the circle and proclaim, "Were you my leader?" in a tone that left no doubt that the questioner felt that they were right! "Are you sure?" the follower would repeat.

The discovery of the gap for themselves between what they believed to be true (who their leader was) and who it actually was that day was significant and bonding across all the diversity in the room. They realized that this challenging reality was true for everyone—it was not limited to one race, gender, etc., and opened up the truth that to really make progress in DEI, we need everyone, and it would be ludicrous to put blame on race, gender, age, or any other specific dimension of diversity. We really are all in this together.

Beyond a Shadow of Doubt

For all the followers (which was everyone—we did two rounds), their unexamined assumptions and perceptions were now recorded, for all time, in their leader drawing. There was no wiggle room to say, "Oh, I never would have thought that about you," or "That thought would never have crossed my mind." Outside of the workshop, these are way too familiar dismissive phrases that those on the receiving end of prejudice and incorrect assumptions are so used to hearing. Sadly, damaging impact from the behavior driven by these unconscious assumptions and perceptions has already been done.

The True Power of Self-Discovery

People have a distinct and powerful reaction when they discover for themselves that their assumptions and perceptions are not always correct. No amount of intellectual persuasion could generate the spark of that emotional moment. "Oh, my goodness, I was so sure that it was you! Are you really sure that it was not?"

"I am."

Elements of an Effective
Adult Learning Model

Building Block 5: "Know the Learning Model" is key here because it gives us an anchor for how we design and facilitate DEI training that will generate real change. The foundational principle of adult learning theory involves allowing people to learn what they want to know and for their own reasons. No two people have the exact same motivation for learning, especially difficult, emotion-laden topics like human differences and similarities.

We try to use multiple modes of learning to account for that fact. Still, as facilitators, we can never know who gets what and why they get it. So, we offer information in the form of learning experiences. We invite participants to be mindful of their discovery (which only they know). We encourage them to determine if that discovery matters to them (Implication). We allow them time to think about how they will change their behavior based on their new insights (Application). Exhibit 2 below illustrates the cycle of learning used for adult learning.

Exhibit 2. Adult Learning Model

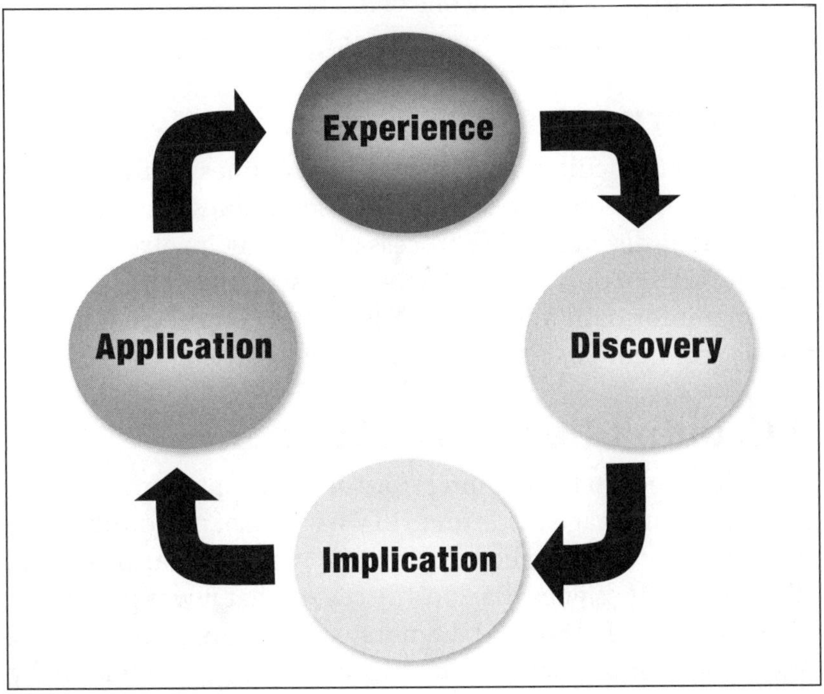

Humans consume information in a variety of formats. It is important to use as many of those formats as possible in a learning session because of different learning styles. That is why we provide multiple modes of presentation for the learning experiences offered to a group. They include:

- Games
- Small group discussions
- Mini-lectures
- Videos
- Personal reflection worksheets
- Models
- Reading prepared content

The Trust Walk was only one of many diverse learning experiences we provided for our group during that workshop.

Discovery

This is where facilitation gets hard. Sometimes facilitators are aware of what people are learning and sometimes facilitators are not in on the discovery. The process of learning involves converting information into knowledge. As a classroom leader, you control what information is shared. You do not control what knowledge is acquired. That is the domain of the learner.

It Couldn't Be a White Woman!

As we described in the opening story of this chapter, my follower, Barron, had an image in his mind of what type of person and style of leadership would make him feel safe in this precarious blindfolded walk experience. Barron's discovery that it was possible to feel that way, even though I did not match his image of someone who could ever do that for him, was very impactful emotionally, and it stayed with him.

Implications (So What?)

Humans adopt knowledge based on new information. Then they must determine if that knowledge has any value for them. That is the "So what?" question. Much of the process of thinking of why a bit of knowledge is valuable comes naturally. The human brain always screens data to determine which is relevant and important and which is not necessary for one's life. This is one of the reasons that DEI training must be powerful and meaningful to individuals and why they must make an emotional connection. Otherwise, there is the grave danger that the whole DEI training experience just becomes an interesting intellectual conversation, but nothing changes in an individual's behavior or in the organizational culture.

Questions like the ones that participants asked at the end of the Trust Walk exercise are vitally important to raise and discuss. The "What if?" questions: "What if I do this in my job? My life?" "What if I am missing seeing talent when it is right in front of me because of my expectations of who and what it should look and sound like?" The powerful questioning of the implications if the same unconscious bias could impact their behavior in their business and/or personal life bears witness to why Building Block 5: "Know the Learning Model," is so important in successful DEI work. They can then begin to apply that learning.

Application (Now What?)

The commitment to behavioral changes begins in the classroom. During all the activity and interactions in the classroom, people begin to imagine how they will use their new insights to experiment with new behaviors for the purpose of developing new habits. The classroom experience gives them a "why" to change. They develop their own "how."

It is not usual for Jim and me and other DEI facilitators who use the adult learning model to hear from participants years later. They still remember that diversity moment when they became aware of some aspect of diversity, equity, and inclusion that had been invisible to them until the experience in the workshop and probably would still be, if they had not had that life-changing DEI training experience.

It Haunts Me Still

When I occasionally ran into my follower, Barron, he would shake his head, laugh, and say, "I realized things about myself and others that I still think about quite often. I will never forget that Trust Walk Experience. The awareness has made me a better manager and person."

Sustainable Learning: How Did We Do It?

The four elements that led to sustainable DEI learning, in the Trust Walk Exercise:

1. *Experience*: The (leader-follower) blindfolded silent Trust Walk.

2. *Discovery*: Things are not always what they seem; I can make mistakes by assuming.

3. *Implication*: I need to be conscious of my perceptions. I need to examine my assumptions.

4. *Application*: How might this process happen in my "real life?" What can I do proactively to manage it now that I know it happens?

The group did good work with the Trust Walk that day. We use it as an example of Building Block 5: "Know the Learning Model," and to remind us that we are all capable of the same behaviors as my follower, Barron—the parts that led him astray, and the DEI leadership behaviors that made him shine.

Building Positive DEI Relationships

Equipping people to have positive, constructive relationships at work is not a nice-to-do business principle. It is a business essential. Attitudes, thoughts, beliefs, and feelings are not the problem, nor are they the target of an effective DEI initiative. There is a saying, "What other people think of me is none of my business."

The target is skills, behavior, practice, and tangible interactions. It is only when negative attitudes turn into negative behaviors that problems occur. You can't hurt me by thinking ill of me. It is when that ill thinking causes you to do something harmful against me that it becomes a problem. For instance, racism is an unconscious bias that affects our decision-making. Decisions inform behavior. When racism turns to racial animus directed at a person or group, it can lead to discrimination. Discrimination is hurtful, expensive, and just plain wrong.

Implicit attitudes do not necessarily predict discriminatory behavior. That is why we lead with behavioral change and allow behavioral change to inform beliefs and attitudes. Again, positive (nondiscriminatory) behavioral norms are good for business.

The Information Trap

Many of the diversity-related training courses now in vogue assume that all participants are, or should be, interested in the topic. There is a large and growing body of knowledge about issues like race, gender, LGBTQIA+, disability, generations, ethnic culture, and other academically inspired subject matter. Participants are encouraged to learn and internalize an ever-expanding diversity lexicon. This imposes unnecessary complexity to the DEI skills development process. It becomes too much for people to internalize. Most people will simply shut down and give lip service to the program. Information is not transformation.

Don't Teach, Facilitate Learning

The key to good facilitation is the ability to get people to create their own knowledge and to own what they create. The facilitator may provide a clear path to a specific learning point, but the learner decides what that specific learning point will be for themselves. Facilitators are classroom leaders, which means they simply point in the direction of the principles under consideration. Real learning takes place when the learner writes or speaks the insight they have developed based on those principles. According to the research, that self-produced learning will stick 90 percent of the time.

Adults Like to Learn, Give Them the Chance

Forcing people to know what you want them to know is a losing proposition. The process of transferring information to others, as in instructing, is fraught with "potholes." As classroom facilitators, we should use what we know about getting others to hear, consider, and understand information we are sharing.

Recent research reminds us that any group of human students has a diversity of background knowledge, personal interests, and values which shape their acquisition of information. An effective communicator must be aware that people ignore most of the information they are exposed to. To be effective, classroom leaders must achieve credibility with the learners and appeal to each person's fears and aspirations.

Fears and aspirations are most likely to stimulate focus and activate memory. We have found that a good technique for stimulating interest is to ask questions like, "How many of you like to think of yourself as a good person?" The natural defense of that self-perception ignites focus when it is in any way challenged or called into question. Many of the exercises we employ invite participants to examine their goodness.

The Type B Question

One practice of good facilitation is the art of developing well-crafted questions that spark immediate responses from the class members. According to Michael Wilkerson, author of *The Secrets of Facilitation*, this kind of question is called a Type B question. It comprises a lead-in, an extension, and a content piece. The lead-in invokes memory or fantasy or aspiration. That lead-in uses words like, "Imagine that you...," or "Remember a time when...," or "If you could think of...." The psychology behind the technique is that every participant has a unique story that derives from a unique set of life experiences. When a speaker is sharing a subjunctive inquiry, each person will imagine a scene from the perspective of his or her own life story. The speaker may be painting a picture from his or her life, but each person is seeing the picture from his or her own life. The more vivid the picture, the easier it is to come up with responses to the final part of the question.

The second part of the process is to extend the image. Give people time to develop a clear picture by adding clarity to the image. This is done with a statement that reinforces the personal nature of the image. For example, after the lead-in you might say, "You are experiencing great success with your idea," or "Your team is now performing at its best." You might even add a kicker like, "Can you see it?" to further invoke the vision.

The third part of the Type B question is the content piece. The speaker asks what she wants to know from the participants. So, instead of asking, "How do we solve this vexing problem?" the facilitator will say, "Imagine that you have just submitted a winning suggestion to management that is going to be used by every team in the company. You are recognized as the developer and go-to advisor on the process. What would you tell people to do?"

Think of a time when you were at a lecture and got triggered by something the speaker said early in the talk. Once your mind got activated by that thought, you likely did not hear most of the talk that followed. What are you likely to remember from that experience—the content of the lecture or the feelings and thoughts that were evoked? That is the psychology behind a Type B question.

Stereotypes

As a human being, you learn to categorize your world from the moment you enter it. Being able to categorize is vital, and it is almost impossible not to do it. It's human. However, it is possible and desirable not to judge the categories as "bad" or "good," but instead to see people as simply different from one another.

Generalizing is related to categorizing. As mental shortcuts, generalizations are helpful. What is not helpful is categorizing or labeling a person as "Black," "White," "handicapped," or "gay," for example, and then automatically making assumptions or decisions about how that individual is likely to behave or what he/she is likely to believe.

Most stereotypes involve negative feelings. If people in a stereotyped group do not meet the expectations we connect to the stereotype, we typically view them as exceptions to the rule, and the stereotype does not change. Only your view of the person you are interacting with changes. Your view of that person has changed because you have established a relationship with that individual. Use DEI training to give participants a safe and supportive place to begin to build authentic relationships with those who are different from them.

Changing stereotypes is very difficult. In many cases, even with reliable evidence to the contrary, people will cling to their stereotypical perceptions. However, we can be more aware of our stereotypes and learn how to manage our behaviors. The best way to manage our behavior with our stereotypes is to question our perceptions or assumptions about the individuals we are stereotyping.

Prejudging (Perceptions and Assumptions)

The Perception Assumption Model (presented in Chapter 4) represents how experience, education, environment, and socialization impact our ideas, beliefs, and personal reality. This also can be the basis for stereotyping people into categories.

When processing assumptions about diversity, your behavior is shaped by the elements of your background, how you were socially programmed in the past, and how you are being influenced today. The way you filter information determines how you interact with people who are like and unlike you.

Our stereotypes and biases are present in the filter box. They affect our assumptions, perceived reality, and eventually, our behavior. The gap between your perception and current reality indicates the need to examine your assumptions and seek additional information before drawing a conclusion.

Understanding the sources of your information and how to better manage your perceptions and assumptions will enable you to develop a more receptive attitude toward those who are different from you within your personal and work environments. The power of social programming is tremendous. How do you think it influences your decisions about others in your sphere of influence at work?

The gap between your perception and the current reality indicates the need to examine your assumptions and seek additional information before drawing a conclusion. Your influence on your employees is strong and important. Isn't it worth a few extra seconds to make sure that your influence is positive and respectful? Develop the habit of pausing before you act. We refer to it as using the "three-second pause" technique.

The Three-Second Pause

In workshops, we have seen how acting naturally can have unintended consequences. You may say or do something that is inappropriate or offensive and that damages your relationship with an employee. Or, you may be saying the right thing, but your tone and demeanor may communicate your true feelings non-verbally. Notice that you may not have any conscious, malicious intent.

To guard against slipping too hard or too often, we recommend a tool called the three-second pause. Surprisingly, in as little as three seconds, you have time to examine your assumptions and modify your reactions so that you can avoid an unnecessary faux pas. During the three-second pause, you should be thinking:

- What am I assuming?
- Why am I assuming that?
- Is it based on old, unexamined perceptions, or is it fresh, real, and validated?
- How am I about to behave? Is that the right thing to do?
- What is the best way to respond to ensure that I am creating a basis for a genuine relationship with this person?

Implicit Bias

Everything contains bias. It is a natural human condition. There are two types of bias to be aware of: conscious and unconscious. As previously discussed, we all prefer certain things and people. That is a conscious bias. We also have a natural leaning in favor of some people and against other people. That is our unconscious bias. We need to discover these biases so they cannot silently and negatively impact our behavior.

There is a now well-known online self-discovery tool from Harvard University called the IAT (Implicit Association Test). It is designed to alert people to their underlying unconscious biases. Those biases result in people making decisions that affect others negatively and they don't even realize why they made the choice in the first place. That is valuable information to have if you desire to be your best self.

Some have challenged the validity of the tool, and some have used it in ways that were not intended. However, in our experience, it has, at the very least, gotten folks talking about the process of making assumptions, unconscious bias, and implicit associations of specific dimensions of diversity with various characteristics; for example, the association of heavyset people with laziness, women with family, men with authority, etc.

It can also become a source of competition which temporarily derails the potential DEI learning as Jim reports below:

(Jim) I was facilitating a DEI session with a medical device and products company. I assigned the entire group, which included the CEO, to do at least three IAT tests as prework for the session. When I asked for feedback on the experience with the tests, the CEO proudly announced that he had won. I asked, "What do you mean you won?" He went on to say that he had repeated one test four times until he was able to get closer to the outcome he wanted (a "better" score). It is important to note that this was a very competitive industry led by very competitive people. So, I finally had to share with him that the intent of the exercise was not to win. It was to learn.

Sometimes the path to "discovery" in DEI training takes a temporary detour, but do not give up. Get back on the pathway to learning and keep going.

Reacting to Differences

It is natural for humans to react to anything that represents difference. Our brains are designed to alert us to potential danger or discomfort. This reaction comes in the form of mental and visceral jolts causing us to pull up and avoid or evade the source of the difference. Differences in other humans is included in this natural brain function. It serves us well to avoid potential danger.

The same natural brain function betrays us when it comes to developing productive relationships. We recommend that everyone develop the habit of turning to curiosity or wonder about human differences. That habit is much better than denigration or condemnation without explanation.

The antidote to this natural reaction to differences is to spend enough time to discover what you have in common with another person (seek similarities). We believe that we can find something in common with any other person on the planet. Once you do, the differences don't matter so much.

The Human Condition

The purpose of effective diversity-related training is to promote new behaviors. It is not to educate people on the broad range of esoteric academic theories that underpin human relations and social change. So that we reach the largest number of people, we need to keep the content as simple as possible.

Rather than the latest theories of race studies, gender studies, sexual orientation studies, social justice constructs, political science, ethnic studies, or other topical areas, the focus should be simply on the conditions we all share as humans. A simple way of expressing them is bias, prejudice, stereotypes, and reactions to differences. That is the human condition that we all share and understand. It levels the field and makes us all complicit in the failure to manage those conditions. What else do people need to know?

The process of learning using the model above is not just for the classroom. Many participants have reported that they have found it useful in every area of their lives. It has improved relationships at home, on the job, in the neighborhood, the community, within their faith community, and in every other aspect of their lives. Awareness is valuable when it translates into new more effective behaviors.

Building Your DEI Training Foundation

In the workplace, DEI should be concerned with creating more comfort and productivity among team members through better human connection and personal behavioral change. It is a simple objective and a simple process. It has fallen victim to the natural group process of overcomplexity. DEI training needs to make us all deeply aware of how the unexamined assumptions that drive our perceptions also impact our behavior. We know that our behavior has an undeniable impact on individuals, business, and society. We recommend using solid adult learning fundamentals (Building Block 5) as the foundation of all your DEI training.

Chapter 7

Experiment—Expect—Examine. Confirm That it Works

"Diversity: The art of thinking independently together"
—Malcolm Forbes

How do you know you have been successful with a training effort? It requires an unusual assessment process. We ask participants if they allowed for movement in their point of view, if they discovered anything of value to add to their personal perspective, if they felt we covered all the areas we discussed at the opening, and if they are committed to continuous learning about people. What else could you expect from a training session?

Training is a catalyst for organizational change. Ultimately, people own the responsibility to change, and, as significantly, the organization owns the responsibility to allow the changes to rise and flourish. Effective DEI training combined with Building Blocks 1 through 6 will help everyone accelerate the desired changes for enhanced business success. Spoiler Alert: There also can be billion-dollar losses if you don't do it right!

What Are You Looking For?

DEI efforts can yield many benefits. One breakthrough idea from a non-traditional employee (a person differing from all other members of a particular group or set) can reap huge financial rewards for any enterprise willing to embrace and leverage the rich diversity of its people. A positive work climate can provide employees with a laboratory for more effective relationship building.

An effective team of diverse composition can outperform more homogeneous teams. The right diversity on a team can make solving any problem easy. However, to reap these benefits you must be willing to experiment with new behaviors (though the change may feel uncomfortable at first), support the proposed changes with positive expectations (negativity can be a deadly and costly force in any business initiative), and examine results with an open mindset. Way too often this is easier said than done, and the DEI value is never given a chance to actualize.

Implicit in Building Block 6: "Know Your Execution Plan," is the commitment to give the DEI plan a chance to work. The right diversity on a team can make solving any problem easy. But to realize these benefits, you must experiment, expect, and examine.

Experimenting in new ways of doing things, and sometimes even just changing behaviors by being more inclusive, can bring up fear and resistance from some people. South African leader Nelson Mandela, who exemplified 21st century transformational leadership of the highest order, had this to say about fear: "I learned that courage was not the absence of fear, but the triumph over it. The brave man is not he who does not feel afraid, but he who conquers that fear."

Breakthrough Thinking

When Julius Pryor was the regional sales manager for a pharmaceutical company, he represented a compound designated and targeted for prostate cancer. Julius boosted the sales of his product line with one obvious idea (obvious to him; blind to the other executives): he suggested to the leaders that they needed to spend more time with Black doctors. But leadership did not see the value.

So, luckily for the business, Julius decided to experiment with the idea. He did the research, collected the data, and conducted a study of the prostate cancer market. It turned out that Black men had a higher incidence of prostate cancer than the general population. While Black urologists made up only 3.6 percent of the urologists nationwide, they were a rich target audience. Equipped with research data and positive expectations, Julius treated this market with the same diligence and respect as all others that he managed.

The good news is that at the final step of Building Block 6: "Examine," the examination of results was impressive. Tapping into the Black doctor's market resulted in more than 20 percent of the total sales of the compound coming from Black doctors in the first year! As a line operation executive, Julius embraced Building Block 6: "Know Your Execution Plan," and made it happen.

Change Happens at the Individual and Team Level

The focus of diversity-related training is on a change in individual behavior developed through human connection and enterprise strategy. Sometimes the best research you can do as facilitators and advisors to confirm the efficacy of DEI is simple observation. We have seen visible and tangible behavioral change in people who have experienced a catharsis, an epiphany, an "aha" moment, or as our colleague Pollie Massey calls it, "movement."

People change in their own way and for their own reasons. When teams change, it is usually because the manager of the team has had an awakening about how the team is managed. The advent of more diversity changes the dynamics of the team and requires the team leader to adjust so that the team delivers its best performance. Much of that change is related to relationship building and combining individual strengths to improve team strengths.

When a manager understands human nature and the human condition, including his or her own humanity, they can better see ways to promote cohesion on the team and to increase team effectiveness. When teams perform better, divisions perform better. When divisions perform better, the entire enterprise will see improvement.

Experiment

One of the most comprehensive studies of the efficacy of diversity management was conducted in the late nineties. The study, entitled *The Effects of Diversity on Business Performance: Report of the Diversity Research Network*, looked at what was working and what was missing for the benefit of diversity management to be realized. Among its key recommendations was the need for more experimentation. Experimentation is needed at the individual, team, and organizational levels to change habits. New habits are formed slowly and only stick when they are properly nurtured.

The Nature of Habits: Changing Personal Behaviors

There's a good reason for habits. If we had to consciously think through every action we took, we'd be exhausted. When we have to consciously think about how to perform any task, it takes mental energy. That wears us out. When we are tired, we unconsciously lapse back to our fast (associative) thinking to conserve mental energy and provide easy, if not always well-reasoned, answers to difficult situations.

If you have a habit of reacting to human differences, it will take deliberate intention to overcome that habit and maintain a new habit of seeking similarities first. Even though you learned the benefits of seeking similarities in your training session, you have to practice it before it becomes natural and sustainable. Once you experience consistently better outcomes from the new behavior, it becomes automatic and feels more comfortable.

To change entrenched habits, we have to find effective replacements, insert them into our daily life, and be vigilant. It takes energy and effort (at first). Even then, you have to be on alert because old habits can be triggered. They don't disappear. They have simply been supplanted with new behaviors. They can and will return if we are not consciously aware of the desire for new outcomes.

The Demonstration Project: Changing Group Behavior

(Jim) Dave Peterson, cofounder of North Highland Consulting, often reminds me that the best way to test an idea to see if it works is to do "one-in-a-row." A demonstration project is designed to confirm the efficacy of diversity management as a strategy and capability. It involves a simple comparison of results from doing things the old way with the old team make-up versus doing things differently with a more diverse team. The measure of efficacy is tangible results and better outcomes, including better problem solving and predictions, cost savings, efficiency rating, and improved safety rating.

Examples of Group Changes

At Neutrogena, a wellness and beauty product company, line managers were trained to plan and execute demonstration (experimentation) projects to confirm the value of broader thinking for improved production. The participants considered the concepts of diversity management as they developed plans to improve their operations.

A demonstration project is a deliberate effort to confirm the value of more innovative thinking from broader perspectives. One breakthrough idea could produce greater efficiencies in production; more accurate prediction could save millions of dollars; better problem solving could accelerate production goals; better decisions could improve quality without added cost. With these intentions in mind, they all created plans to test production the old way (standard teams and routine processes) against a reimagined production process (more diverse teams and openness to change).

John Deere, a company that manufactures agricultural equipment and machinery, adopted a diversity management strategy in the early 2000s. They intended it to be a value creation tool for their operations. Instead of sending the usual suspects to DEI conferences, John Deere experimented by regularly sending a large contingent of line operations managers. Those line managers went back to John Deere and executed their production tasks with an awareness of the principles of DEI.

The head of DEI at John Deere was a member of the Advanced Practitioners Think Tank. She reported that line managers were recognized at John Deere as the source of value creation. The company felt it was imperative that those managers understand and practice diversity management principles to help John Deere maintain its competitive position.

Expect

(Jim) In my last business book, *Managing Differently*, I introduced my readers to the Belief System of Motivation and Performance developed by Dr. Thad Green. The Belief System is based largely on the expectancy theory first proposed by Vic Vroom. The simple idea is that people will be motivated to perform if they know that performance will be recognized and rewarded.

If a company invests wisely in effective foundational diversity-related training, it has a right to expect that its people will perform differently. The people who participate in that training have a right to expect that the principles of diversity management will become a part of the daily practice by workers, managers, and leaders. It is only reasonable to expect people to demonstrate new behaviors if their work environment rewards the new behavior and not the old.

When diversity management is approached as a strategy rather than a reaction to pain or gain, the desired outcomes are established up front. In some cases, that means that people will be required to practice dignity and respect toward all employees and customers, that managers will build teams with positive relationships among all team members, and that team results will reflect a higher level of cohesion and performance. Behavioral expectations should be evident in how people make decisions, solve problems, collaborate, innovate, socialize, and produce.

Expectations at Work

In 2000, Georgia Power did an assessment that revealed a pattern of aberrant behavior that popped up about every ten years. In each case, some manager failed to live up to the standards that were consistent with his or her strong "family" culture. When aberrant behavior happened in the past, the company responded with intense focus on the issue followed by corrective action on the case, and a quick return to normal business (stop, fix it, and move on). That response is exactly the way the company managed all major disruptions, such as power outages. They would alert all employees to be ready, and mobilize all their resources to focus intensely on the area of outage, they would work diligently until the outage was corrected, and then quickly return to normal day-to-day operations. That approach works extremely well when you are dealing with tangible products and services. It does not work when the problem deals with human relationships.

In the case that popped up in 2000, David Ratcliffe (then CEO) decided to break the pattern. He rejected the call to "shoot" (reprimand or fire) the offending managers and instead embarked on a thorough analysis of the culture, a company-wide collection of ideas for improvement, and a learning platform that focused on "valuing differences" and "managing differently." He approved implementation of all the ideas suggested by employees as a gesture of appreciation and trust. He communicated the findings of the culture analysis and the continuous improvement campaign to all employees and reiterated the expectations that all employees treat each other and customers with courtesy, dignity, and respect. Every employee, including all executives, attended valuing differences training and every manager attended managing differently training.

Then, and only then, Ratcliffe asserted the idea that anyone violating the behavioral norms of the enterprise could be subject to removal from the family/company. This initiative was a multi-year, focused approach, in which every executive, manager, and employee felt some level of investment in the effort. Individuals and teams felt equipped to manage their behavior to meet the requirements of the enterprise as outlined in the learning experiences, and as put forth by the CEO. Here's what happened:

- In the past two decades, there has been no repeat of the former pattern.
- There is seldom a mention of the word diversity, except in its very successful supplier diversity program.

- The strong family culture is still evident, except now all employees feel like full members of the family.
- Executives work daily to deserve the label of "most trusted leaders in the industry."
- Workplace relationships, as indicated by engagement surveys, consistently rank above industry norms.

The goals of the change effort seem to be on target. And as a by-product of that effort, the senior operating leadership team of Georgia Power, who were all White men in 2000, are now more diverse at every position, and there is now a Black CEO.

Examine

An adage says you should "Inspect what you expect." It is not enough to let people know what the new expectations are regarding practicing the principles of diversity management learned in the diversity training session. Employees should be invited and encouraged to attend diversity training. They should be allowed to share the insights they learned and examine the impact it had on their work life. Leaders and managers should then find multiple ways to communicate and reinforce the behavioral norms that are expected, based on the principles of diversity management introduced in their diversity training.

The key is to demonstrate that the principles explored in the training are the expected norms of the enterprise for teams and individuals. These norms should be established during the early phases of the change management process. Training should be the vehicle through which people discover and explore how to live up to those norms. But leaders have to examine behavior to confirm that people are living up to those expectations.

Diversity management is a change effort. It requires discipline to make the change stick. Leaders can and should install change with an eye toward sustainability (making it stick). While organizational culture is relatively intractable and there should not be an attempt to change the core culture, the behavioral norms are mutable and should be the target.

The Experiment—Expect—Examine Cycle

The biggest factor in determining the effectiveness of a diversity training effort is the level of experimentation. Experimenting with new behaviors in a controlled setting can quickly confirm the benefit of comfort with diversity and the advantage of being aware of the impact of bias, prejudice, stereotypes, and reactions to differences. The immediate benefit occurs at the individual level, and it can be felt at the team level when managers are equipped to manage diversity and promote the value of diversity. The benefit can be felt across the enterprise when senior executives use their own stories to illustrate how they have been helped by the experiences of more involvement with diversity.

The Cost of Faulty Execution, or "The Apple That Was Never Picked"

The failure to effectively practice Building Block 6: "Know Your Execution Plan," can have monumental consequences. History has shown us that, even in the areas where diversity is less obvious, lack of proper execution is costly, as in the case of non-traditional White men. When non-traditional White men look, talk, and act differently from most White men in an organization, they become the subject of the diversity conversation. We sometimes forget that DEI principles are just as important in this case as ever!

(Laura) "I am not sure we would have even wanted the business of Apple Computer anyway...," stated a clearly defensive senior executive who was throwing out counterarguments to every point made about DEI in our workshop. An equal opportunity offender, he directed his comments to all of our statements by facilitators and participants alike.

We were discussing the famous story of Steve Wozniak and Steve Jobs, cofounders of Apple Computer, when he made his declarative statement about "not wanting the business anyway." The DEI relevance of the story, possibly a tad embellished with folklore mythology, nevertheless is very real with a less than positive ending for Hewlett Packard (HP). Many of the clients we work with today are not aware that Steve Wozniak was an employee working for HP before joining up with Steve Jobs to create Apple Computer, one of the most successful companies ever. Wozniak presented several personal computer ideas to HP, but they were never picked for development. Let's explore and learn from what happened.

HP had an Engineering Review Board whose purpose was to screen new technological ideas from enterprising employees for things like viability, market acceptance, and funding. The Engineering Review Board was a homogeneous group from similar backgrounds, and with similar looks and clothing style: picture White men, clean-shaven, Ivy League graduates, expensive suits, and wingtip leather shoes. It is fair to say that, at the time, and possibly even now, Steve Wozniak, a longer-haired, bearded, and much more casual dresser, who had already dropped out of Berkeley, did not fit the image of the powerful affinity bias within the HP Board. In fact, Steve's ideas were consistently ignored. So the DEI question arises: Was it the way Steve Wozniak looked, his job level, his lack of formal education and/or overall "packaging" that impacted the Engineering Review Board's decision to not act on his ideas? Or were they just incredibly incompetent? Or both?

Don't Deny—Rethink

Then there is the added challenge to DEI growth from situations like this one. It is the challenge of those not willing or wanting to acknowledge and examine the reality of the situation, to gain DEI skills and learning. Examination is critical to making sure that they do not make the same DEI mistake again.

The dynamic of the initial denial and/or refusal to discuss potential DEI missteps often is familiar to experienced DEI facilitators who go deeply into these DEI issues with folks. On that day, a senior executive made the borderline ludicrous statement that "We [HP] would not have even wanted the business of Apple Computer anyway." Seems a bit hard to believe. What company would willingly deny an opportunity to be on the ground floor of a business that, years later, has over $200 billion dollars in the bank and an international presence second to none?

Rather than looking for the golden DEI learning point here, the executive is stuck in trying to prove that he is right—a classic barrier to potential DEI learning and growth, a barrier to which we all are vulnerable. So we all heard his point and offered this question to consider: "Fine, but wouldn't you want to be 100 percent sure that you had listened with an open mind and that the decision of the Board was made on the basis of the technology and not the person's appearance?"

Learn

The invitation to learn from this situation for all of us is to consider: "How does this apply to me and our organization, and who are the potential Steve Wozniaks in our company?" It is a chilling experience to hear it. History bears out the truth of our losses due to ignorance and/or lack of quality diversity training. It tells us what we missed. In this case, the loss is extraordinary talent.

This scenario can happen to any of us. The Board acted naturally, without a diversity lens. We can improve by practicing the Experiment–Expect–Examine process to uncover our blind spots, so we make better decisions. We can and must do better with this. Steve Wozniak left HP, teamed up with Steve Jobs, cofounded Apple Computer, and as they say, the rest is a very profitable and successful history.

The Training Link

When you experiment with solid and simple facilitated diversity -related training, you should expect to see a difference in individuals and in teams. If you are looking for the benefit of a DEI effort, start by looking at the individual level and then the team level. If you look first at overall firm performance, you may miss the real change, and you may conclude that DEI and diversity-related training don't work.

But a positive training experience will not produce desired behavioral change unless there is a change in the environment to which people return. The intent of the training is to generate learning that produces change. The purpose of the follow-up plan is to create an environment that acknowledges, welcomes, and rewards the new behaviors. It takes a deliberate, intentional execution plan to pull that off. Humans are creatures of habit. Even after a breakthrough learning event, which alerts us to a better way of being, our tendency is to "lapse back to natural." The old ways will creep back if we are not deliberate in replacing them with new ways. That deliberate process involves experimenting with new behaviors, expecting new outcomes, and examining for better results.

Chapter 8

It Could Happen to Any of Us

"I raise my voice not so that I can shout but so that those without a voice can be heard. We cannot succeed when half of us are held back."
—Malala Yousafzai, 2014 Nobel Peace Prize Laureate

A composite illustration of how leaders, managers, workers, and customers benefitted from the advent of diversity-related training. Vivid examples of the impact on individuals, teams, CEOs, officers, and customers. Based on real world observations and actual verbatim reactions to the experience of diversity-related training in support of organizational strategy. Results are measured in improved team cohesion, excitement and more engagement, a more attractive work environment, avoiding disruptions, more innovation, improved customer relations, and seamless change efforts.

Seek Success

The positive effects of diversity training are greater when training is complemented by other diversity efforts and conducted over a significant period of time. DEI effectiveness is achieved through process. One of the success factors of DEI training is the alignment of the intent, context, content, and delivery of the training. We express that alignment in terms of motive, method, message, and metrics. Misalignment of these elements of a change effort can derail the effort. Here are a few examples of how alignment occurs.

The Motive

In the case of Texaco and other companies, the impetus for a strategic focus on diversity-related training was pain. That pain came in the form of a major high-profile discrimination lawsuit. The response to that pain was a large-scale change effort intended to make sure the incident that precipitated the pain never occurred again. Other companies, like Energen Corporation in Alabama, saw an opportunity to gain from the pain of others by being proactive and addressing the issues that caused others pain before those same issues showed up at its doorstep.

Still others, like many of the early adopters, including Avon, Boeing, Corning, Digital Equipment Corporation (DEC), and GM, benefitted from enlightened leadership and adopted a strategic motive for acting on diversity-related issues. The strategic response was intended to position themselves for the inevitable increase in the magnitude and the range of diverse employees and customers. They chose to anticipate change rather than react to change. It was important to be honest about the motive and to be honest about the response.

The Method

Whatever the motive, companies that engaged in serious diversity management as a change effort followed an established and proven path to effectiveness that mirrors our recommended Six

Building Blocks model. That path included elements such as executive education to develop a compelling "why" for the effort, a culture assessment to confirm how to approach the effort in a way that would stick, and foundational training for all employees to learn the attitudes, skills and knowledge needed to execute and sustain a DEI mature work environment.

At Georgia Power, CEO David Ratcliffe and his Management Council took time to engage in several learning sessions, including an offsite retreat where DEI was the sole topic of discussion. Each executive was alerted to pay attention to his or her behaviors and learn better language skills so that they could represent the company's new behavioral expectations. Later, each of these executives sat in a DEI learning experience as a regular employee along with other employees from every level in the company. Later, they were tasked with serving as opening speakers at the subsequent DEI learning sessions where they revealed their personal journey with understanding and experimenting with new behaviors. Their leadership was often the thing that converted some reluctant participants into willing participants.

The Message

A communications campaign cannot be disingenuous. It will not help if you promote the idea that diversity, equity, and inclusion efforts are aimed at improving workplace climate while training people on obscure academic concepts and measuring results by counting numbers of demographically-diverse hires. Tell the truth and make the case with stakeholders (mostly employees) whose genuine support is necessary for success.

The messaging about the DEI training is also important for success as people enter the training room and/or participate in the "buzz" in the office about the diversity training. Participants must be able to honestly say that they were treated with dignity and respect, regardless of race, gender, or any other dimension of diversity.

The "shaming and blaming" game may temporarily make some people feel better (an outlet for rage and anger from all these dimensions, but ultimately, as Laura's mentor Paul Bracy so often reminds groups, "We were all born into this, none of us created this, our job is to understand it and fix it." The facilitators for Texaco did that, though it was not always easy. The importance of the moment was clear, and in many ways, the world was watching.

The Metrics

Almost without exception, the most important metric for international enterprises is better performance. In business, that means increased revenues, lower costs, an increase in innovation, more efficiency in production, and greater sales per employee. For nonprofits and governmental agencies, that means more delivery of mission-related services. These metrics should be targeted for the team level, not the firmwide level.

For every well-managed team that benefits from DEI and performs at peak levels, there are still others who underperform and allow diversity to be a distraction rather than a catalyst for high performance. DEI efforts get derailed when leaders announce that the effort is a strategic change initiative and yet all the metrics are akin to affirmative action measures.

Feet to the Fire with the World Watching: Vulnerability Equals Strength

(Laura) One of my most memorable DEI experiences. Which personifies much of what we are talking about in this book, was at one of the biggest companies on the planet at the time, Texaco. Here is a bit of what was so special.

The executive conference room was full of diversity consultants recruited from many different backgrounds, all sitting in the seats normally filled with the CEO's homogeneous White male executive staff. As the CEO entered, I thought to myself, "Give the man credit—at least he showed up."

Texaco, the company he led, was faced with a racial discrimination lawsuit that was all over the international press. Indisputable tape-recorded evidence had surfaced, and initial settlement demands were well over 500 million dollars. The CEO, Peter Bijur, walked into our facilitator meeting room wanting to learn. That is a place from which we can always begin—and so, we did.

A team of over twenty elite diversity trainers had been hand-picked for their level of expertise and experience in DEI work. Our mission was to help the company address the now very public toxic DEI environment in the company. The company had operated on the "informal affirmative action plan model" that few beneficiaries wanted to talk about. This unwritten cultural norm consisted of actions, procedures, and informal/unwritten rules and procedures that had benefitted and served well-connected Caucasian men for decades, and enabled environments that protected and advantaged them for years.

During that time, people not "in the club" (women, non-Whites, less privileged Whites, etc.) were consistently and systemically passed over for jobs that they were more than qualified for, were treated with disrespect, and had no allies with any organizational power to support them. In fact, frontline workers who suggested improvements to the operations were explicitly told, "We hired you from the neck down. Remember that." In addition to all the other destructive "isms," (racism, sexism, homophobia) raising their ugly heads in the company, classism (discriminatory behavior based on "socio-economic" class), sadly, was prevalent as well.

The CEO looked at Jim, me, and the others, and stated, "We need help. I need help. Where do we start and how can we do this? I want real change." We could sense his authenticity.

The company got lucky that day. The right people, in the right place, at the right time showed up. Using the concepts outlined in our Six Building Blocks, including the essential commitment from the top levels of the organization, the supporting structure for diversity training that generated real change was put into place. This structure included a brilliant and ethical HR manager, Ed Gadsden, charged with managing the diversity training component of the lawsuit settlement. Gadsden knew the value of and need for behavioral change. A team of experienced diversity trainers who believed in Zen facilitation was assembled. There was also a commitment to diversity training for all levels of the organization, clear goals and objectives for the DEI work, and management and employee accountability.

The approach was inclusive of all dimensions of diversity. No one, no difference, was to be blamed, shamed, or left behind. As stated in a case study about Texaco presented at the National Academy of Engineering in 2002, the company's leaders insisted that the reforms would not be targeted solely at salaried African Americans (i.e., the class-action members), but would be extended to address the rights and needs of all employees, including women, White men, and all minority group members. Short and longer-term plans for the diversity initiative were tied to business strategy and goals, and plans were made for a diversity, equity, and inclusion review of hiring processes, employee development, training, and vendor selection. In addition, a diverse panel was established to track progress.

Keys to Success

The companies that achieved some measure of success with DEI had several things in common. Their approach was based on business and strategic imperatives. They were not coerced into taking action. They were serious, not just curious, about the potential of diversity, equity, and inclusion. Based on their experience, here is a model for effectiveness on the diversity journey.

Start at the Top

The executive leadership team at the companies that made serious efforts with DEI recognized their unique position as role models and chief advocates. They engaged in a sometimes year-long process of educating and reconditioning their thinking to understand and then promote the value of diversity and inclusion in their enterprise. These leaders learned to be vulnerable and solicit feedback from employees as they developed their capacity to see and use diverse talent more efficiently and effectively.

Each executive was alerted to pay attention to his or her behavior and learn better language skills, so they could represent the company's new behavioral expectations. Later, each of these executives sat in a DEI learning experience as a regular employee, along with other employees from every level in the company. Later, they were tasked with serving as opening speakers at the subsequent learning sessions, where they revealed their personal journey with understanding and experimenting with new behaviors. Their leadership was often the thing that converted some reluctant participants into willing participants.

Assess the Current DEI Environment

The beginning of any successful DEI effort requires thorough diagnosis or assessment. Any organizational development practitioner will tell you that "Prescription without diagnosis is malpractice." DEI assessment involves two major pieces of research: a culture analysis and diversity readiness.

A culture analysis is meant to clearly articulate elements of the existing organizational culture so leaders can plan how to conduct the change effort in a way that will not be rejected by the masses of employees. As we know, culture is the ruling factor of organizational life. It is relatively intractable, and it involves a lot of rules that are unwritten and unspoken. Understanding an organization's culture can increase the likelihood of success with change significantly (over 70 percent of change efforts underperform or fail).

When Johnson & Johnson's Consumer Products Division embarked on a DEI effort, the members of the Leadership Council authorized a culture analysis (or culture scan) to help them manage the implementation process more effectively. Of course, the results of the culture scan did not reveal anything that they did not suspect or know. After all, they had all thrived under the current system by being able to navigate that culture.

The culture analysis gave credence, words, and measurable data, including a baseline metric, to their gut feelings about what was acceptable and unacceptable at J&J. One of the leaders in that group expressed surprise when she saw a particular characteristic of the culture. She said, "I knew that was true about us, but I have never taken that into account in the way I manage meetings." Having access to descriptive language allowed the leaders to manage projects and people more efficiently and avoid the numerous built-in traps of navigating the natural reactions to change. This is where attention to Building Block 3: "Know Your Audience," becomes even more evident.

The diversity readiness assessment provides an opportunity to get direct input from employees about the viability of and energy for a DEI change effort. Using information from surveys as well as focus groups, you can get a real sense of what employees would expect from such an effort, and what they recommend so it is successful. As a recent internal DEI practitioner put it, "We spend so much time sitting around a table, trying to figure out what to do, when all we have to do is ask."

State Your Intent

Children's Healthcare of Atlanta (CHOA) constructed a statement that is consistent with its mission and the direct experience of its White female chief executive officer and Black male chief operations officer. At CHOA, diversity, equity, and inclusion is not a reputational add-on; it is an essential element of enterprise performance.

Ron Frieson, now the Chief Operations Officer at CHOA, has the advantage of having been the first executive to have the official title of chief diversity officer when he was with BellSouth. He knows the difference between "window dressing" (words with no meaning or substance behind them) and statements of reality (what is really happening in the organization). The key part of CHOA's DEI statement has elements of the original definition of diversity management and is conceptually clear to all of its constituents.

> Children's is built upon appreciating and valuing the differences and similarities that exist in the collective mix of employees, the patients and families we serve, and the communities around us. We will strive to create an environment where people feel valued for their professional and their personal contributions, and where the mix of these contributions is unlimited. We will deliver the same high level of service and respect to each of our patients and their families. And by enhancing the lives of all the people touched by our organization, we will enhance the lives of the children we serve.

Notice that the words "diversity" or "inclusion" do not appear. Those words do not add clarity to CHOA's intent. More importantly, this DEI statement aligns with employees' experience. Still, the principles of diversity, equity, and inclusion are at the core of the message.

It is common for organizations to develop and publish a glowing statement that indicates its desire to become diversity friendly and diversity mature. If you read the diversity section on any company website, you will see those types of statements. Most of them are empty platitudes that repeat what others have said. Serious players construct their statement based on their personal recognition of the messy, sometimes uncomfortable, but vital role DEI will play in their long-term success as an enterprise.

Commit to Real Change

Serious players learn enough about the potential and the process of creating a diversity mature enterprise so they can make an intelligent and well-considered decision to commit to it. We said earlier that it is unwise to make a half-hearted attempt at DEI efforts. Failure at DEI can set your company back by a decade before it is safe to raise the issue again. The backlash, loss of trust, and demoralization from empty efforts can be that destructive.

When internal DEI practitioners tell us their chief executive officer is committed, we often will ask, "Committed to what?" Jim's mentor, Dr. R. Roosevelt Thomas Jr., often said (based on years of working with C-suite executives), "It is easy to be committed when you don't know what you are committing to." Earnest commitment includes a recognition of the need, the process, the investment, and the expected outcome of a serious DEI effort. It will require the strength to be vulnerable, but the return on the investment can be remarkable.

Use the Multiday Model

The beauty of the multiday diversity training model is that people get to witness each other's attitude and behavioral changes. It is a memorable, and sometimes phenomenal, experience. The changes are, in part, the result of colleagues sharing a spectrum of stories about the impact of differences on their life experience. The spectrum ranges from being misjudged, to robbed of opportunities that would have made an easier life for them and those they love, to violence resulting in death. Feelings of despair, anger, frustration, rage, hopelessness, and depression often filled the training room.

After a day of hearing others and telling their own truths, participants almost always made an emotional connection to the principles of diversity, equity, and inclusion. There was often a marked difference in how people "showed up" the next day. People treated each other better.

Some even dressed differently, having a renewed sense of pride. For example, at Texaco, frontline workers would often show up on the second day in shirts and ties rather than their typical work clothes—because now they felt like somebody worthy of respect and with a renewed sense of dignity.

The catalyst? From facing each other with their deepest feelings and shared stories in the training sessions, a foundation of understanding, empathy and compassion had developed. It gave most participants hope and strength, and a sense of commitment to make real DEI change.

In this circle of trust and acceptance, the often-painful conversations had created a bond that turned "suspicious enemies" into "cross-difference allies." New friendships were born, and people reported that they "could never look at the world in quite the same way anymore." This is how powerful and impactful behavioral diversity training done well can be. Similar to diversity programs, diversity, equity, and inclusion training done well (formulated from the Six Building Blocks), also produces good results. As Laura so often states, "If you open your head and heart to diversity, equity, and inclusion, you'll get a wisdom and a richness that by definition you cannot get any other way."

Make It a Requirement for Leadership

In the near future, comfort and competence with diversity of all types and inclusion as an enterprise norm will be non-negotiable. The increasing flood of diverse talent and diverse customers will require leaders who manage diversity, equity, and inclusion naturally, without distraction. That change includes dealing with a new generation of employees for whom diversity, equity, and inclusion is not an anomaly; it is an expected attribute of the world and a desired condition of the workplace. Leaders of any age who struggle with the inevitable change in the landscape of business and society (including the increasing diversity of the workplace and marketplace) will become obsolete.

Train for Behavioral Change and Management Skills

The training component of the change process should have clear distinctive objectives. The serious players often set out to: 1) clarify new behavioral expectations and equip people with the tools to change as needed; and 2) equip managers with skills to get the best from teams of diverse composition. Knowing what the training targets are makes it more likely you will hit them. That involves both a foundational learning experience for all employees (Experiential: Building Blocks 4: "Know How to Deliver" and 5: "Know the Learning Model") and a strategy of providing DEI management skills training for managers and leaders (Building Block 6: "Know Your Execution Plan"). Depending on the size of the enterprise, this step takes several years to complete.

Promote Continuous Learning

In nearly every case, the serious players instituted a DEI learning series after the foundational DEI training. That included town halls led by senior executives and more formal instructional DEI-related training. The Office of Diversity Management at Georgia Power established a library for those who wanted to continue their learning about diversity management. They also conducted a series of additional training sessions that related to the new behavioral norms. One of those sessions was about retaliation. Others related to the workplace climate that they had set out to establish. Each senior executive also made a point to include diversity, equity, and/or inclusion as part of his or her speeches and in memos to his or her departments.

Keep It on the Agenda (for the Right Reasons)

Meeting protocols were a great way for companies to reinforce the key DEI messages. All meetings at Texas Instruments manufacturing began with a safety review. Safety was a core value and talked about incessantly. At many of the most successful companies, DEI was given the same importance, and was a required topic at every meeting. Every executive team meeting had a section dedicated to updates on diversity, equity, and inclusion management.

Company newsletters had a section focused on diversity learning. Several ERGs (Employee Resource Groups) were formed with a DEI focus. Annual engagement surveys included questions about the climate for DEI. It became natural to have candid discussions about diversity. Without these follow-up activities, DEI training can become a one-and-done event with limited impact.

Expect No Guarantees

Even doing all the right things for the right reasons doesn't guarantee long-term success. Fifteen years after the groundbreaking book *In Search of Excellence* by Tom Peters, half of the companies featured as exemplars in the book have faltered, lost market leadership, been acquired, or gone out of business. More recently, many of the companies highlighted in Jim Collins's book *Good to Great* have also fallen out of greatness. Mastering and benefitting from diversity management and diversity-related training now will not guarantee you will sustain that benefit going forward unless you continue to improve in your DEI practice.

The Training Philosophy

Several companies we worked with have made serious efforts to implement diversity management as a part of their strategic mix. They chose to give the same level of interest and effort to DEI as they did to all other strategic issues.

Training is an important part of any strategy implementation. The role of training is to provide a common understanding of the issues and to create personal commitment to the strategy. No short cuts. No excuses. No reactions to outside forces. It took serious consideration of all the factors that make for successful DEI training efforts, beginning with the right philosophy.

As such, the following considerations are incorporated into our training designs.

Attractive Experience

DEI training should be an event that creates positive anticipation with managers and other employees. It must have impact and be perceived as fun rather than a "heavy trip." The earlier sessions, including the pilot, can be used to develop some positive "folklore" about the program that will make all future participants anxious to be involved. DEI issues are deathly serious, but serious and solemn do not have to go together in every aspect of DEI training. The fact is that when people are relaxed and having fun, they are often more open to DEI learning and having the essential conversations for DEI understanding and growth.

Tied to Strategy

Diversity training, and all other training for that matter, should have a clear connection to the key strategies for success. Part of our challenge is to make sure the sessions we produce are linked to the strategies that senior management is talking about.

Based on Values

Nothing in our program should be in obvious conflict with core values. If the organization has articulated its values, then they will be incorporated into the DEI design.

Clear Objectives

Since training can cover so many areas, it is imperative that we focus on achieving the DEI outcomes that are most important for these sessions. To do that, we must know our objectives and stay true to Building Block 1: "Know Your Why."

Identify Holes

It is well worth the time to do sufficient diagnosis to determine what skills, attitudes, and behaviors are most needed and most lacking in the target audience. Sessions should focus attention in those areas where the greatest DEI impact can be realized.

Recognize Culture

The character of all training should be consistent with the dominant culture of the organization. Accommodating the cultural norms of the group makes it easier for them to accept and apply the DEI points that are being offered.

Establish Buy-In

Steps should be taken up front to get support from key opinion leaders in the organization for the DEI training concepts. Participation does not translate into effectiveness unless the participants are open and receptive to the ideas being presented. We aren't just going for giving information—our goal is behavioral transformation.

Follow-Up

Training is a tool for establishing expectations about diversity, equity, and inclusion, as well as opening the channels of dialogue. The benefit of training is greatly enhanced when management reinforces the points regularly. We provide additional information and material that management can use to make sure the issues remain fresh and active in the work groups after the sessions.

Producing Effective Learning Design

(Laura) At Texas Instruments, the DEI design process involved a team of design engineers from inside the company and from expert advisors. The team began by agreeing on a desired outcome and a set of DEI objectives. That information was combined with knowledge of the culture and indicators from the diversity readiness research. Next, the team considered what technology was available to help achieve those outcomes. Technology included games (that trainers play), models, informational narratives, company statements of strategy and values, and executive communications. These components were then compiled into a process flow that allowed for effective consumption of information and development of knowledge. The final product of this step is an annotated outline of the learning experience with potential (flexible) time estimates.

Development

Development of a training product involves the production of the physical means of conducting the training. That means assembling the models, videos, narratives, games, group interactions, and other tools. The end product of this process is a complete participant guide and a facilitator manual with tools included.

The next step is to conduct at least two pilot sessions to test the effectiveness of the design in a live session. There will invariably be instances where pilot facilitators discover a need to change the flow, rearrange segments, and add or eliminate a module.

While the learning experience is being packaged and tested, the internal training administrator would develop the means to populate each class with the best mix of participants. We normally request that each class have as broad a mix of diversity as possible. That includes race, gender, ethnicity, sexual orientation (if known), executives, middle managers, frontline workers, support people, and occasionally an outsider. Often that means access to an employee database and development of a program that identifies a random selection of participants based on the diversity mix.

Delivery

In preparation for the delivery phase, serious players often sponsor and conduct a training of facilitators (TOF). We always invite experienced and skilled practitioners to be a part of the training project. Still, they need the extra preparation to make sure the learning experience is consistent and properly focused.

It begins with a personal greeting from a company executive. For example, Peter Bijur, CEO of Texaco, greeted our faculty and made it clear that: 1) he appreciated our involvement; 2) he needed our help; 3) he would do his part to support us; and 4) there were unique elements of his company's culture, values, and strategy that we needed to know to be seen as credible.

Understanding the uniqueness of the client group was as important as mastering the content and flow of the learning experience. When the training was launched at Texaco, it was with great fanfare and a sense of positive anticipation. The top senior leaders would often announce that they would be in a class early in the process without saying which class. As each group of participants left the sessions, they were encouraged to share how they felt about the experience without revealing too much about the actual content.

The facilitators were considered a part of the learning community at these sessions. As such, they also experienced new discoveries about people and about themselves. We required our facilitator teams to engage in and mediate a debrief of each session by providing quality improvement observations to each other. They would share: 1) what they liked about the other's leadership; 2) what caused them to wonder; and 3) how the other could be even more effective in the future. That mutual sharing helped maintain a consistently high-quality experience from the beginning to the end of the delivery cycle.

Debrief (Follow-Up)

There is something called a "glow" following impactful training. People experiencing effective diversity-related learning generally feel good, positive, inspired, and sometimes agitated. They want to test their new learning back in the workplace. Unfortunately, the "glow" doesn't last forever. When people are faced with the reality of the day-to-day whirlwind of business, they often lapse back to their natural behavioral patterns. This unfortunate outcome can be avoided.

It is important that the behaviors and skills discovered in a diversity-related training session be reinforced in the workplace. This reinforcement is the responsibility of managers. Managers have inordinate influence on the work life of every employee. A good practice for managers is to spend time with each employee one-on-one. This practice is especially useful as an individual returns to work after an immersive learning experience.

The manager should sit down with that employee and ask, "What did you learn?" and "How do you plan to use that discovery in your work group?" Then the manager should reveal his or her own learning from the training and indicate how it has changed their behavior. Managers should make it clear that they will be looking for and monitoring improved relationships on teams, based on the DEI training. This sends a powerful message that real change is expected and is an important goal.

Conclusion

Start, Restart, or Recover: But Get on Track

Hope against hope. We need to believe that someday, somehow, we will finally master the behaviors that create an equitable society. We make small movements in the right direction only to lose ground later. In many cases we have the right social strategy but lack the capacity to execute.

The Journey Begins

We strive for a tipping point when all our good intentions result in an irresistible pull toward right actions. We wait for the next generation to get it right. The one key element of change we tend to overlook is benefit. Change happens when everyone sees greater benefit from the new way as compared to the old way.

Many analysts suggest that diversity training does not work. It is clear from the negative press about diversity training that there is a severe lack of understanding about the intent, the context, the desired outcomes, the design process, the strategic focus, the delivery modality, and the content of effective diversity-related learning experiences. At the same time, there is heightened awareness in the world about the inequities of social justice. A history of a visible "caste" system that plays out in destructive "isms" around the world is becoming better understood.

There is a call around the world for corporations, institutions, and other organizations to stop being part of the problem and to become part of the solution. Effective DEI training is a critical component of any DEI strategy and can be part of that solution. This book answers the many questions of how to make diversity training work to meet its goals as a necessary tool to answer that call.

Use the Six Building Blocks and the other models and concepts presented to support your DEI journey. We never said that it would be easy, but we do know that these tools can and do work. We hope that in moments of weariness, despair, and even joy at a DEI breakthrough moment, you will reach out across differences to find anchors, comfort, acceptance, and ultimately, a human connection that understands, and you know is standing right there with you.

Sustainability

We have seen the interest in DEI rise and fall and have witnessed numerous efforts to refresh the field, primarily by changing the language and condensing the approach. DEI is a marginalized topic in many organizations. We believe it is important that leaders understand the value of DEI in business success (the commercial possibilities of an effective DEI effort), as well as the importance of corporate/organizational social responsibility. Diversity training needs to support both of those needs. This book reflects that orientation.

There has also been a lack of reporting on the extraordinary success that individuals and organizations have experienced based on effective diversity learning. We have offered diversity learning experiences for over thirty years in enterprises of all types and sizes. This type of training has powerful and meaning-ful results because the focus is always on:

a) human connection and behavioral change

b) sound adult learning theory

c) organizational strategy and success

Without these components, you are checking off the box for sure, but do you really believe that it is changing behavior for the better and is the best way to deliver DEI training? Or is it a quick, easy, and cost-effective tactic not intended to generate real change?

Facing Frustration and Despair

We know the frustration experienced by practitioners who know the limitations of other approaches. We know the despair of those committed to true DEI change when they are faced with the guarded disinterest of corporate leaders who fail to do the work necessary to make DEI an essential part of company strategy. We have all seen the disgust expressed by employees who sense that once again, nothing is going to change. The frustration and de-spair are why this book is needed now.

An often-quoted concept states that, "When the student is ready, the teacher will appear. The teacher can light the way, but the student has to walk the path." The need is great to help people truly walk the path of diversity, equity, and inclusion in all aspects of their organizations. This book is designed to help the "student" walk the path.

More than ever, individuals and organizations are proclaim-ing that they are ready to walk the path. They are hungry for DEI training that will truly help them make significant prog-ress on the lifelong journey of DEI learning. A "teacher" has ar-rived in the form of this book: *Diversity Training that Generates Real Change: Inclusive Behaviors that Benefit Individuals, Business, and Society.* However, all these great ideas are meaningless unless they are acted upon. *Who will you be?*

So, What if You Don't?

So, what is the risk of doing nothing? The risks are many and they are significant. We now have the research to prove that, as many DEI practitioners have known for a long time, candidates evaluate the evidence of diversity, equity, and inclusion policies, practices, and training as they research companies and through the interview process. Research from Glassdoor for employers tells us that "More than 3 out of 4 job seekers and employees (76 percent) report that a diverse workforce is an important factor when evaluating companies and job offers."

In addition, it reports that "Employees increasingly seek to hold their employers accountable to live up to their pledges to become more inclusive." The bottom line is that whether or not your company is interested in increasing its diversity, equity, and inclusion, most candidates are nevertheless evaluating you on it and making decisions at least partly based on that data.

For these and so many other reasons, we need to bring back the soul to diversity work through DEI training that makes human connections and promotes behavioral change. So many have joined Black Lives Matter and other movements demanding that the world wake up, face the injustices, and take meaningful action. The corporate social responsibility statements in annual reports need to be more than words on a page.

A History of Incompleteness

One of Jim's executive friends from AT&T once told him, referring to diversity awareness training, "OK, we are aware. Now what?" Jim was told about a diversity project manager at GM who challenged the diversity management consultants by essentially saying, "We appreciate the appetizer. We are ready for the main meal. What should we be doing differently?"

Those challenges went unanswered for many years, which accounts for the initial demise of diversity management as a staple of business management. The issue, in essence, is how do we move from theory (concept) to practice? That open question made it likely that the movement would get distorted, distracted, co-opted, and derailed. We can (and need to) do better. The Six Building Blocks lay out a proven path to success.

Reduce the Rhetoric, Work with What Is Real

Diversity, equity, and inclusion training should avoid the false impression that marginalized or underrepresented groups are looking for special treatment or playing by a different set of rules. The constant barrage of special programs for women, minorities, and other identifiable populations (except White men) distracts us from the simple goal of the DEI movement, which is comfort and productivity with any other individual, and to see everyone as equal.

The litany of special efforts on behalf of all non-White males compounds the two major barriers to success: White guilt and minority victimhood. The great American musician and philosopher James Brown said it best: "I don't want nobody to give me nothing. Open up the door. I'll get it myself." The American system of democratic capitalism depends on that philosophy. Anything that violates that principle will produce failure and cannot be sustained. In the past, violation came in the form of suppression, oppression, first-mover monopolies, preferential treatment for the dominant class, and assumptions of lower expectations for some groups.

Today that violation comes in the form of political posturing, reliance on programs for advantage, social division based on artificial differences, and distorted concepts of freedom. Thirty years ago, with the prospect of the shift in demographics becoming evident, a Puerto Rican scholar, Sam Betances, expressed it this way: "White people have done a great job building this house of abundance (American capitalism), but you can't build it alone anymore. Let us (growing non-White populations) help you."

The prospect of the inevitable shift to a nonmajority White society (the multiracial, multiethnic democracy) produces fear in many, simply because it represents a major change in the look and feel of American society. If we could relax and recognize that we are one, and that no group means any harm to any other group, we could continue to thrive.

Go Forward

Wherever you are on your DEI journey, we recommend that you proceed this way:

Back up. Stop and take stock of your current position as well as the landscape of the business environment. Make choices based on good solid business reasoning rather than symbolic gestures or public posturing.

Think strategically. Review your current competitive positioning. Ask yourself if a people strategy like diversity management is a good idea for this company. Would a serious DEI effort benefit employee, customers, other stakeholders, and even the financial health of the enterprise? Can we win with DEI?

Spend wisely. Jim's father always said, "Buy quality (expensive) clothing and they will last for years or buy faddish (cheap) clothing and have to replace them every six months." Spending on shortcuts in your DEI efforts is a waste of money. If you spend a little to check the box you will need to repeat the process again and again. If you instead invest in a serious DEI change effort, including effective diversity training, you will benefit from it for years to come.

Pre-sell the idea. Before you announce that you are presenting any type of diversity-related training, make sure you have declared and demonstrated why you are doing it. Let people see that the leaders have embarked on a serious journey of learning for their own development. Then allow the people to share in that learning journey.

Focus on personal growth and behavioral change. Reject the urge to latch onto the latest topical information dealing with any dimension of diversity. The real work of DEI is simple and replicable. Equip people to understand human nature (others and their own) and help them develop the capacity to manage their instincts in favor of reason. The more they know, the more they will act with comfort and an appreciation of human connections.

Get help. It is popular now to use only internal resources to manage the DEI efforts. Most leaders will freely admit they don't know what DEI is or how to do it. Unfortunately, they then assign the issue to people who are equally unaware of the potential of DEI or the proven process of executing it well. There are many resources available to help you get off to a good start. Working really hard while doing the wrong things will still leave you where you started.

Conduct a culture analysis. Edgar Schein, the father of corporate culture, said, "The number one job of a senior executive is to manage the culture." Culture is the primary driver and primary blocker of effective change. Overlook it at your own peril. A thorough understanding of the organization's culture can increase the likelihood of success with change by a significant degree.

Define why. "First things first" (Covey). "Begin with why" (Sinek). These and other bits of organizational wisdom have helped many enterprises thrive amid rapid change. That same wisdom applies even more to the idea of embarking on a serious DEI journey. First ask, "Why does this make sense for this enterprise at this time?" You want to know what the benefit will be if you do it well, and what the penalty will be if you fail. Don't just do something. If you are not convinced of the need or the potential for good, do nothing.

Outline outcomes. When companies embarked on efforts like TQM (Total Quality Management) or Six Sigma, they had clear expectations of the outcomes. Their intentions were to increase yield, improve customer satisfaction, lower costs, improve efficiencies in production and delivery, and reduce cycle times. What are your expectations of your DEI efforts? You should expect to see access to more and better talent, more efficiencies, more innovation, better problem solving, better retention of talent, more creativity in product development, more and quicker team cohesion, reduced costs, higher sales and revenue, and other intangible benefits that translate into higher performance. You will never get these benefits unless you expect to.

Make it a valuable and desirable experience (non-punitive). What could possibly motivate any employee to willingly participate in a diversity-related learning experience? The answer is always that they can see some personal benefit in it. If you are conducting or sponsoring diversity-related training, you need to make sure it is apparent to participants that they will benefit personally. Rather than mandate attendance, provide incentives for engagement. That means letting employees or members know how their new behaviors will be rewarded in the organization. It doesn't hurt if everyone has heard good things about the experience so that they can't wait to be included.

Make it "uncool" to not participate. No one wants to be an outlier. You should adopt the language and principles introduced in diversity-related training and make those messages ubiquitous in your workplace (newsletters, word campaigns, executive speeches, memos, other broad communications, etc.). Make sure the language you adopt is inclusive language, not exclusive language in support of any one dimension of diversity.

Reinforce the learning with behavioral expectations on the job. Leaders (business, political, social) set the behavioral expectations of any group of people. When those expectations are consistent with the principles of diversity and inclusion, it reinforces the importance of the insights people develop during their learning process. When people know that what they learn will be used regularly, they are likely to study, practice more diligently, and strive toward mastery.

We Can Change

Like nearly everything in life, this book has bias. We recognize that diversity-related training has expanded to have broader reach than in the past. Our primary focus remains with the application of these principles to training sponsored and conducted by business enterprises. We believe that individual growth, business value, even social change, should be led as much by business leaders as by politicians or social activists.

Leaders must understand that the goal is not to change attitudes and beliefs—it is to change behavior. Race is not the problem. Discriminatory behavior is. That is why diversity management advisors never suggest that diversity training is designed to change beliefs. The purpose of the course is to invite people to behave differently. What you think of me is none of my business. I only need to know that you treat me with respect and dignity. The golden rule that is foundational to all major religions does not say, "Feel (or think) about others as you would have them feel about you." Instead, it says, "Do unto others as you would have them do to you." It is about behavior.

As experienced practitioners of diversity management, we encourage our clients to change their behaviors and practices.

We make it clear up front that the purpose of a diversity learning experience is to address inherent bias and to provoke people to manage and control the impact of their biases. We do that by introducing bias as a fact of the human condition, and by offering insights into the cause, the impact, and our capacity to manage bias. The incentive for managing bias, prejudice, and stereotypes is always connected to corporate strategy and the behavioral expectations of the company culture.

We advise leaders to say, "When you sign on to work here, you agree to put your beliefs in check and treat all the employees and customers of this enterprise in a way that preserves a positive relationship with both." Why? It's good for business. Granted it is also more humane, compassionate, and indicative of goodness. But in business those are the by-products of behavior that preserve customers and engage employees. We start by insisting that corporate leaders share what they know about the efficacy of diversity management based on results, not rhetoric.

In Closing, Wisdom and Richness

Diversity training done well brings a richness and wisdom that people and enterprises could not get any other way. As Laura says, "If you open your head and heart to diversity, you will bring a wisdom and a richness into your life that by definition you cannot obtain any other way." The same is true for individuals, businesses, and society.

• • • •

This is a unique moment in time. Political and government leaders of all stripes are particularly receptive to meaningfully addressing racial animus and changing behaviors in all aspects of our economic and community relationships. The sustainability of this moment will be determined in large part by whether our corporate leaders decide to walk the talk. It will take more than pretty words on their websites and in public Zoom meetings. It will require presence and action in the hallways of Congress, state capitols and our courthouses. It will require business leaders to exercise leverage, courage, and strength of character beyond their historical comfort zone. It is time. The promise of diversity, inclusion, and social justice hangs in the balance.

Diversity Training That Generates Real Change

Discussion Guide

Key Concepts

- DEI is a relationship discipline
- For success, use interactive, facilitated, experiential training, based in adult learning theory
- Training is a key part of the execution plan, not the whole plan
- Done well, training accelerates change; done poorly, training can derail change efforts
- Like any other business initiative, use clearly stated, realistic goals, and effective measurement tools
- DEI training should be based on strategy, adult learning concepts, and inclusion

Our hope is that *Diversity Training That Generates Real Change* will be a valuable resource to you and your organization. The Discussion Guide uses the Six Building Blocks as a template.

We have identified key questions for each building block and encourage you to add your own. The more that you can customize the concepts to be easily and effectively applied to your organizational culture, the better chance you have for diversity training that will generate real change. We encourage you to experiment, expect, and examine with an inclusive mindset using your head, heart, and hands as you continue on your DEI journey. Use this Discussion Guide with senior executives, human resources, the DEI office, your work team, community groups, and others. We are cheering you on!

The Six Building Blocks

Building Block 1 (Chapter 2)	Know Your Why
Building Block 2 (Chapter 3)	Know Your Strategy
Building Block 3 (Chapter 4) (Adults)	Know Your Audience
Building Block 4 (Chapter 5)	Know How to Deliver (Facilitation)
Building Block 5 (Chapter 6)	Know the Learning Model
Building Block 6 (Chapter 7)	Know Your Execution Plan

Study Guide Key Questions

Building Block 1 (Chapter 2)   Know Your Why

1. Why have you decided to embark on DEI training?
2. What are your key objectives? Are the objectives realistic and doable?
3. What are we trying to accomplish through the training?
4. What would success look like?

Building Block 2 (Chapter 3)   Know Your Strategy

1. Are the training objectives clearly linked to business strategy?

2. Are the facilitators fully briefed on how to link the workshop material to business strategy?

3. How will you reinforce the DEI concepts covered in the training to business strategy outside the workshop?

Building Block 3 (Chapter 4)   Know Your Audience (Adults)

1. Are the exercises designed on solid adult learning concepts?

2. Is there a good balance of experiential exercises and other types of learning tools (small group discussion, self-reflection, case studies, etc.) that support adult learning?

3. Can the learning objectives in each exercise be applied directly to business strategy?

Building Block 4 (Chapter 5)   Know How to Deliver (Facilitation)

1. Are the facilitators skilled in self-discovery style (Zen) facilitation?

2. Are the exercises designed for adults to direct their own learning?

3. Is there sufficient time built into the training design for group discussion of key concepts?

Building Block 5 (Chapter 6)   Know the Learning Model

1. Is the workshop overall design in alignment with the Learning Model: Experience—Discovery—Implication—Application = Sustainable Learning?

2. Are individual exercises designed using the Learning Model?

3. Are the training objectives inherent in the Learning Model exercises?

Building Block 6 (Chapter 7)   Know Your Execution Plan

1. Does your Execution Plan include all Six Building Blocks?

2. Who will be accountable for each part of the Execution Plan?

3. How will you measure success?

Acknowledgments

Jim and Laura

Gratitude and thanks to Steve Piersanti, Berrett-Koehler editor, for his belief in us and this book.

We are also grateful for our colleagues and clients who have taught us and others so much, for all kindred spirits who, despite the challenges, work for diversity, equity, and inclusion in their own ways every day, and for all the courageous DEI leaders, past and present, on whose shoulders we all stand.

Laura

For me, writing this book was a much more isolating and solitary experience than I expected, so I want to acknowledge and express my gratitude to my friends, family, and colleagues, who understood and supported this dream all the way along.

A special thanks to my sister, Arlene, for her 24/7 support; to Stephanie and Stephen Child, for their faith and boat rides; and for Mary Church, who insisted that every milestone in this process was worthy of celebration! Deepest thanks and gratitude to my friend and beloved colleague, Jim Rodgers, for inviting me along on this journey at just the right time.

Index

About the Authors

Jim Rodgers and **Laura Kangas** have worked together for over twenty-five years. Their differences are a valuable asset to their partnership, and it allows them to produce better solutions for their clients. As a consulting team, they exemplify the power of deliberate diversity. This book is the result of their hours of deep discussions about diversity, inclusion, and equity issues.

Jim Rodgers, PhD, FIMC, is recognized as a thought leader and the leading strategist in the field of diversity management. As the president and principal consultant of The Diversity Coach, he provides high-end executive coaching, DEI advice, and counsel to senior executive teams from major corporations in all industries.

Dr. Rodgers has a unique perspective about the intent and content of diversity efforts in business, government, nonprofits, and the academy, borne from his experience as a former corporate executive. A thirty-year proponent of diversity management and a research scholar of diversity management, he has an intention "to promote the value of diversity and to reduce the stigma of diversity."

Dr. Rodgers has provided advice and counsel to over three hundred executive teams, including several dozen chief diversity officers, and an equal number of CEOs. He has written extensively about workplace dynamics and the power of diversity management as a strategy and an organizational capability.

His book, *Managing Differently: Getting 100% From 100% of Your People 100% of the Time*, was praised for changing the conversation about diversity management and was recognized as one of the top fifty books to read by Thinkers360. In addition, Dr.

Rodgers was elected as a Fellow of the Institute of Management Consultants (IMC USA) and hailed as a Top 50 Thought Leader for Organizational Change by Thinkers 360.

Dr. Rodgers is also a spiritual teacher and a serial nonprofit leader. He has served as board leader with organizations like Habitat for Humanity (Atlanta), Ecumenical Ministries of Newark, Literacy for All (Georgia), and the High Museum of Atlanta. He holds a BSEE from Howard University, an MBA from the University of Alabama, and a PhD in Management from Walden University.

Laura L. Kangas, MA is a global organizational and management development consultant, workshop and program designer, facilitator, speaker, and writer. For over twenty-five years, she has collaboratively developed strategies and leading programs in diversity, equity, and inclusion, and other areas of individual and organizational development. Her clients include Texas Instruments, Pfizer, Microsoft, Massachusetts General Brigham, Partners Healthcare, Southern Company, Boston Scientific, Fidelity Investments, the United Nations Credit Union, The Harvard Graduate School of Public Health, Neal & Massy Limited (Port of Spain, Trinidad and Tobago), The Vernā Myers Company, and many others.

At Pfizer she was a member of the executive team that developed the strategy for DEI training for the top two thousand managers globally. Kangas helped design the training, trained the trainers, and led sessions around the world. At Texas Instruments, Kangas and her team designed and delivered DEI trainings to all three shifts and consulted on DEI strategy. At Neal & Massy Limited she designed and delivered the first Global Leadership Program on the islands of Trinidad and Tobago. Kangas was recruited to join the team of DEI elite facilitators during the ground-breaking Texaco $500 million racial lawsuit in the late seventies. She was also one of fourteen international facilitators at the Parliament of the World's Religions in Chicago in 1983. International bestselling South African author and journalist Kate Turkington dedicated a chapter about Kanga's life in her very popular book *Doing it with Doris*.

Prior to her consulting career, Kangas was a program manager for diversity and inclusion at Digital Equipment Corporation (now Hewlett-Packard). She and her team designed and delivered DEI training to more than 150,000 employees around the world. Kangas received several awards from the company for her contributions to HR and DEI.

Kangas has a great respect for academia, which is why she regularly designs and teaches courses at many colleges and universities, including the Boston University Graduate School of Public Health, Lesley University, Becker College, Webster University, the International School of Management on the Isle of Man, and the Accelerated MBA Program at the Shanghai University of Finance and Economics, Shanghai, China.

Kangas developed the Perception Assumption Model that is widely used by diversity practitioners and organizations as a game-changing framework for understanding unconscious bias. Her work at Hasbro with Center Focus International received a national award from the Society of Research Management for creativity and innovation in diversity training design and facilitation.

A passionate traveler, Kangas holds a MA from Harvard University and a BA from the University of Massachusetts at Amherst, Massachusetts.

Dear reader,

Thank you for picking up this book and welcome to the worldwide BK community! You're joining a special group of people who have come together to create positive change in their lives, organizations, and communities.

What's BK all about?

Our mission is to connect people and ideas to create a world that works for all.

Why? Our communities, organizations, and lives get bogged down by old paradigms of self-interest, exclusion, hierarchy, and privilege. But we believe that can change. That's why we seek the leading experts on these challenges—and share their actionable ideas with you.

A welcome gift

To help you get started, we'd like to offer you a **free copy** of one of our bestselling ebooks:

www.bkconnection.com/welcome

When you claim your **free ebook**, you'll also be subscribed to our blog.

Our freshest insights

Access the best new tools and ideas for leaders at all levels on our blog at ideas.bkconnection.com.

Sincerely,

Your friends at Berrett-Koehler

Certified

Corporation